THE CLINICIAN'S
MANAGEMENT HANDBOOK

The Management of Health Care

Series Editors
John J. Glynn and David A. Perkins

Published:

Managing Health Care

Edited by John J. Glynn and David A. Perkins

Other titles in the series:

Managing Health Service Contracts

Achieving Value for Money

The GP's Management Handbook

THE CLINICIAN'S MANAGEMENT HANDBOOK

Edited by

David M. Hansell

Clinical Director of Imaging, Department of Radiology,
Royal Brompton Hospital NHS Trust, London

and

Brian Salter

Reader in Public Policy, Centre for Health Services Studies,
University of Kent, Canterbury

WB Saunders Company Ltd

London   Philadelphia   Toronto   Sydney   Tokyo

W. B. Saunders Company Ltd 24-28 Oval Road
London NW1 7DX

The Curtis Center
Independence Square West
Philadelphia, PA 19106-3399, USA

Harcourt Brace & Company
55 Horner Avenue
Toronto, Ontario M8Z 4X6, Canada

Harcourt Brace & Company, Australia
30-52 Smidmore Street
Marrickville, NSW 2204, Australia

Harcourt Brace & Company, Japan
Ichibancho Central Building, 22-1 Ichibancho
Chiyoda-ku, Tokyo 102, Japan

A catalogue record of this book is available from the British Library

ISBN 0-7020-1915-1

Typeset by Paston Press Ltd, Loddon, Norfolk
Printed in Great Britain by WBC, Bridgend, Mid Glamorgan

CONTENTS

CONTRIBUTORS

William Bain Chief Executive, Royal Brompton Hospital, London, UK.

Peter Barnes Consultant Physician and Cardiologist and Executive Medical Director, Hope Hospital, Salford, Manchester, UK.

Jennifer Cowpe Unit General Manager, Royal Brompton Hospital, London, UK.

Glenn Douglas Director of Finance and Information, The Medway NHS Trust, Chatham, Kent, UK.

Kim Hodgson Director of Business Development, The Medway NHS Trust, Chatham, Kent, UK.

Richard L. H. Long Secretary to the Trust, North Kent Healthcare NHS Trust, Keycol Hospital, Kent, UK.

Kingsley Manning Visiting Professor, The Management School, Imperial College, London, UK.

Anthony J. Newman Taylor Consultant Physician, Royal Brompton National Heart and Lung Hospital, London, UK.

Ronald Parker Consultant Surgeon, Surgical Directorate, Walsgrave Hospital NHS Trust, Coventry, UK.

David Savage Independent Management Consultant, London, UK.

Colin L. Smith Senior Lecturer in Medicine, University of Medicine, Southampton General Hospital, Southampton, UK.

FOREWORD

Jenny Simpson

Doctors are, essentially, practical people. Their basic approach is to make things work using whatever tools are to hand. Whilst medical training provides an impressive body of clinical knowledge and theory on which to draw, doctors know that every patient is unique and will respond uniquely to known therapies. Medicine is without doubt a science. But it also retains an element of craft, and wisdom. Intuition and empathy are as critical as knowledge, analysis and theory. In many ways this continual balancing—between the pragmatic and the theoretical—positions doctors to be ideal managers.

Management decisions are equally unique. Skilled managers learn to balance scientific analysis with intuition and empathy in steering complex human endeavours. Nevertheless, management became a foreign territory for many doctors and as recently as ten years ago one could find little, if any, writing on medical management published in the UK. Perhaps this is why some of the earlier works aimed at doctors involved in management happily attempted to cover the entire domain in only a few chapters. A smattering of finance, a paragraph or two on personnel, a sketch of the NHS and there you have it.

Fortunately, for those of us deeply involved in the development of clinical management, the broadening and continued development of the literature is beginning to provide much more mature examples. I feel sure that this handbook will truly live up to its name. Each chapter not only provides an overview of a specific management area, as well as some practical insights, but also, and much more importantly, begins to provide routes into the more substantial bodies of management knowledge available under each of these headings.

I see *The Clinician's Management Handbook* sitting within easy reach of the clinical director's chair, flanked on either side by a growing number of specialist volumes, some of which are referenced in the chapters, as clinical directors develop and expand their own managerial style and competencies. For some, individual chapters will provide all the necessary information to fill knowledge gaps and to provide an insight into the points at which help from say, finance or personnel professionals is required. Others may want to turn to the more technical studies on, for example, the different approaches to costing and their particular strengths and weaknesses in specific situations.

Just as this book provides a consolidation of earlier, more hesitant, writings on clinical management, so the continued emphasis of the vital management role of the clinician, evident in circulars and documents throughout the service, acknowledges the reality that whatever further reforms there may be to the health-care system in England, the continued place of clinical professionals in the management of the service is not in question. The growing numbers and managerial sophistication of the members of my own organization provide solid evidence of the increasing impact and influence of clinicians in management throughout every healthcare institution in the UK.

The growth of management literature for doctors and the growth of doctors in management are of course interlinked and inter-twined. This volume—a judicious blend of doctors' writings with those of academics and management specialists—signals a greater degree of openness and a significant change in attitude towards management on the part of clinical professionals. These doctors gain respect for continuing to practise clinical medicine whilst grappling with the complex issues of management. They also gain respect from management colleagues for the unique contribution that they can make, as equals in the management process. From uneasily straddling a fence, clinicians in management are taking up a critical link position between two converging worlds. For if managers and clinicians are to share the same vision, then it is those people, particular clinical directors and medical directors who straddle the two worlds, who will be best placed to articulate those visions and provide the leadership, the setting of values and the inspiration so essential to the NHS.

Jenny Simpson
Chief Executive, British Association of Medical Directors

INTRODUCTION

David M. Hansell and Brian Salter

Until recently it was assumed that the management of clinical activity was the prerogative of the medical profession. The prevailing view was that doctors alone should decide what doctors did. However, a series of changes in both policy and practice have combined to challenge this assumption. National Health Service (NHS) managers no longer accept that the exercise of clinical autonomy can be conducted without regard to organizational and budgetary considerations and, increasingly, are prepared to confront those doctors who maintain such a stance. As a result clinicians today face a choice: they must either acquire the knowledge and skills to manage more effectively or they must accept that others will try to do it for them. As Ron Parker graphically puts it in Chapter 1 of this book, 'we either lead or we are led'. In this introduction we analyse the pressures which have challenged the presumed medical leadership of the NHS and the reasons why effective management skills are a means of maintaining it.

THE PRESSURES FOR CHANGE

The fundamental political issue facing the NHS is that there is, and always will be, an infinite demand for health care and a finite supply of resources. In the past this rationing function was handled covertly and discreetly by the medical profession, the public accepted clinicians' decisions and there was no serious pressure for the efficient management of scarce resources. Throughout the 1960s and 1970s both patient activity and real expenditure rose at an average of one or two per cent per year and all appeared well.

During this period clinical autonomy was regarded as an absolute right and was largely unchallenged. The 1972 report *Management Arrangements for the Reorganised Health Service* stated the obvious when it observed that 'doctors and dentists work as each others equals and ... they are their own managers'. The report continued: 'In ethics and in law they are accountable to their patients for the care they prescribe and they cannot be held accountable to the NHS authorities for the quality of their clinical judgements' (DHSS 1972, para 1.18). Choices about priorities in patient care were relatively straightforward because there was sufficient flexibility to allow this to be done informally by individual clinicians. Hospital managers, or administrators as they were then known, were kept at arm's length. Indeed, some argued that clinicians should not participate in hospital management at all since this was likely to compromise their medical judgement (Chant, 1984).

Several factors combined to bring this state of affairs to an end. Demand for health care outstripped supply to a degree which generated a long-running debate about under-funding in the NHS. Stimulated by the increasing proportion of elderly in the population (a particularly high cost area), constantly rising expectations about the standard of health an individual should expect and enjoy, and advances in medical technology, demand rose faster than the real increase in the NHS budget. At some point this was bound to raise questions about doctors' unfettered control over the distribution of NHS resources and the 1983 inquiry into the management of the NHS, chaired by Sir Roy Griffiths, was the first sign of things to come. Griffiths argued that there should be a greater emphasis on clinicians' involvement in management because:

> *Closer involvement of doctors is ... critical to effective management at local level.... Their decisions largely dictate the use of all resources.... They must accept the management responsibility which goes with clinical freedom. This implies active involvement in securing the most effective use and management of all resources (DHSS 1983, 18–19).*

It is a sad fact of life that policy recommendations are rarely implemented with the same conviction with which they are stated and Griffiths was no exception to this. Despite the support of the central initiatives by Management Budgeting and Resource Management, both intended to give clinicians the appropriate information with which to manage, little changed. The explanation is simple: doctors had no incentive to take on management responsibilities nor was there any sanction if they did not do so. So why bother?

With the 1989 NHS Review and the 1990 NHS and Community Care Act a fresh political agenda emerged containing the answer to the last question. The final objective of these reforms was to fragment and decentralize the established bureaucracy of the NHS through the introduction of an internal market based upon purchaser agencies and provider Trusts. Trusts were to have a range of powers and freedoms not available to the old health authorities and, in particular, 'should be free to employ whatever and however many staff they consider necessary' depending upon their service needs (DoH, 1989, p. 25). Since their service needs would in turn depend upon their performance in the internal market of the NHS and their ability to attract contracts from purchasing agencies, so also would their requirements for medical staff.

The effect of these changes is that there is pressure for the autonomy of clinicians to become contingent upon the corporate interest and performance of their employing Trust. In theoretical and increasingly practical terms this means that there is pressure for clinical decisions to be related to the contractual commitments of the Trust, for clinical activities to be integrated with its management structure and for clinicians' employment contracts and conditions of service to be adjusted to suit the Trust's corporate needs.

Faced with this situation, clinicians have a choice. They can adopt the ostrich strategy and hope that the new schema is short-lived. Or, they can actively defend their territory by acquiring the skills and knowledge which will enable them to manage in the ever-changing health service. The reader will find the contributors to this book tend to the latter view: this book is designed to help clinicians develop, as well as defend, their territory.

USING THE HANDBOOK   This book is designed to fulfil a variety of needs. The reader may be a junior doctor, consultant, medical director or, who knows, chief executive. It is not intended to be read cover to cover but to act as a handbook that can be dipped into as and when the need arises. Should the reader then wish to explore a particular area further, a short list of texts for further reading is given at the end of each chapter.

The opening chapter by **Ron Parker** is very much the work of an enthusiast committed to the involvement of the clinician in management – as one would expect from the chairman of the British Association of Medical Managers. It provides an historical overview of the increasing pressures for the involvement of clinicians in management and discusses the potential range of roles for a doctor. The following chapter by **Glenn Douglas** and **Richard Long** deals with the statutory and legal responsibilities of the doctor in management, and gives a plain account of the practicalities and pitfalls open to anyone with managerial responsibility in the NHS. In Chapter 3 **Glenn Douglas** unravels the web of NHS finance in a way designed to provide practical guidance to clinicians who find themselves managing a budget for the first, or second, time.

If NHS finance is complex, NHS people are doubly so and in Chapter 4 **Peter Barnes** shows how this complexity can be understood and how the clinical manager can act as motivator and team builder. Then there is, of course, the organization itself and in Chapter 5 **Jenny Cowpe** analyses how organizations operate and how the clinician manager can use that knowledge to influence an organization's direction.

At the core of the internal market in the NHS is the contracting process. Since this determines what resources are available, the clinician cannot afford to ignore it and in Chapter 6 **Kim Hodgson** explains how the clinician can have an important role in contracting in terms of preparation and negotiation. Change in service provision is an integral part of the new NHS and Chapter 7 by **Kingsley Manning** shows how the clinician can take an active role in developing clinical services and achieving a competitive advantage. In Chapter 8 **David Savage** follows this up with a practical step-by-step guide to the use of project management as a means for achieving organizational change.

If clinicians are to manage their services effectively and efficiently they need to know how to evaluate them. Chapter 9 by **Tony Newman Taylor** and **Bill Bain** provides a wide-ranging discussion of the techniques available and their application to clinical services. Finally, **Colin Smith** in Chapter 10 addresses the Scylla and Charybdis of the ethical issues involved when a clinician takes on an active management role, particularly in the context of the pressures exerted by the internal market.

REFERENCES

Chant, A.D.B. (1984), The National Health Service: Practising doctors should not manage. *Lancet* **i** (8391), 1398.

DHSS (1972), *Management Arrangements for the Reorganised Health Service*. London: HMSO.

DHSS (1983), *NHS Management Inquiry*. London: HMSO (Griffiths Report).

DoH (1989), *NHS Consultants: Appointments, Contracts and Distinction Awards*, Working for Patients, Working Paper 7. London: HMSO.

THE MANAGEMENT CHALLENGE

Ron Parker

Ron Parker

OBJECTIVES

- ◆ To examine the nature of the increasing pressures for the involvement of clinicians in management.

- ◆ To outline the main organizational components of the management of clinical services.

- ◆ To identify the key management roles for doctors and the career opportunities therein.

INTRODUCTION

Most doctors are deeply idealistic from the time they leave medical school until the time of their retirement and beyond. Just a few lose their vision but they are the minority. The rest work unstintingly for the cause: for the good of their patients. The same is true of nurses, and other healthcare workers.

Driven by this commitment it is easy to see how doctors become angry and hurt at patients' complaints and political criticisms. There they are, struggling in the front line and behind there is the rising din of comments about inefficiency, waste of resources, delays in outpatients, long waiting lists and the rest. It is natural for them to take all of these barbs personally. There is the feeling that the demands made upon them are unreasonable. 'It is like being asked to make bricks without straw', a colleague once said.

Yet a moment's thought would lead many of these clinicians to conclude that however good many parts of the NHS were they were never properly coordinated and managed to form an efficient organizational whole. It is like a car kit; all the parts are there and in working order but they are not assembled properly. In addition, health care itself is changing in a way that demands ever increasing integration. The NHS could have continued to work in this ramshackle way if resources were plentiful but as financial constraints became apparent its shortcomings were thrown into relief.

Public criticism of the NHS in the early 1980s reached such a level that political action was inevitable. The result was the Griffiths Management Inquiry commissioned by Mrs Thatcher's government. After several months of intensive scrutiny of the NHS the Griffiths Management Inquiry Report (Griffiths, 1983) was presented. It was brief and its adoption by the government heralded the radical changes which have been continued ever since.

SOME PROBLEMS IN THE NHS IN THE PRE GRIFFITHS ERA

Before considering the Griffiths recommendations it is worth looking with the retrospectoscope at some of the major managerial problems within the NHS which the report addressed.

First, there was the separation of the responsibilities for spending from those of managing the budgets. Doctors' decisions generally led to expenditure but without any budgetary responsibility. Administrators, as they were then called, were held accountable for managing the budget but had no control over the spending. This bizarre arrangement would work while there was a bountiful cash flow; as soon as there were financial constraints it was bound to lead to shortfalls and result in late and drastic managerial reaction such as the closure of wards.

A second serious problem was the hierarchical organizational structure. The hospital was responsible to the district health authority which itself was responsible to the regional health authority. This again was responsible to the Department of Health. Within each discipline (such as medical, finance, nursing, administration) there was a pyramidal management structure and many of these stretched all the way to the Department of Health with representation at each level. Decision-making was by consensus and taken together with the hierarchical structure this led, at best, to good decisions disastrously delayed and, at worst, to no decision at all. Such a system was unable to produce a rapid and flexible response to any demand let alone those of a rapidly changing world.

Another barrier to effective management was a striking degree of professional tribalism. Rather than teamwork there was an entrenched sense of independence of each discipline. It is hard to see how such a rigid system could produce the best possible services for the patients and for the nation.

In addition, there was a dearth of good information. It was symptomatic; there was a welter of data but much of it was difficult to apply in managing the service. It had been produced by many people for a wide range of purposes and in many different forms. Much of it was useless.

Finally, John Yates, in his book *Why Are We Waiting* (1987), analysed hospital waiting lists. He found, for instance, the provision of hospital beds for general surgery and urology could be anything from 2 to 17 per 10 000 of the population and the number of consultants, senior registrars, and registrars, taken together, in the same specialties, could vary from 1 to 10 per 100 000 of the population. There was no obvious correlation between the shortage of beds and the length of waiting lists.

As Roy Griffiths commented, 'If Florence Nightingale was carrying her lamp through the corridors of the NHS today she would almost certainly be searching for the people in charge' (Griffiths, 1994).

THE REFORMS

The Griffiths NHS Management Inquiry 1983

Roy Griffiths was concerned about the lack of accountability in the NHS and recommended the introduction of a general management function. Full discussion of issues would still be needed but instead of petering out in the quagmire of consensus there would now be a single general manager who could make a decision.

The report also emphasized that 'responsibility should be pushed as far down the line as possible to the point where action can be taken efficiently'. This particular recommendation was not picked up by the government until later (Griffiths, 1992).

Another important element of the report was its view that 'the NHS lacks any real continuous evaluation of its performance. Rarely are precise management objectives set: there is little measurement of health outcomes; clinical evaluation of particular practices is by no means common and economic evaluation of these practices is extremely rare'.

The report also recommended a need 'to involve clinicians more closely in the management process' (Griffiths, 1983).

A picture was being painted of an organization which should be flat rather than hierarchical, which would set itself clear objectives and measure its performance against these and which would involve clinicians in its management process.

The Resource Management Initiative

The Resource Management Initiative (RMI) was launched by Ian Mills, the Director of Financial Management in the NHS in 1986 (HN (86) No 34). Its overall aim was to 'help clinicians and other managers to make better informed judgements about how the resources they control can be used to better effect ... to result in measurable improvement in patient care'.

Although the initiative came from the Department of Health it was intended that it should take root and flourish at ground level. Accordingly, six hospital pilot sites were established to develop a concept of Resource Management. The whole project was managed by the Resource Management Unit in the Department of Health and the intention was to roll out the initiative to other sites at the appropriate time.

The overall aim of the Resource Management Initiative was further developed and restated 'to enable hospital doctors, nurses, and managers throughout the NHS to adopt better patient care ... and to take more informed strategic and operational decisions' (*Managing Clinical Services*; British Association of Medical

Managers *et al.*, 1993). Clinical and managerial professions were all to collaborate and form teams to take both operational and strategic decisions. The concept was based on the original vision of Roy Griffiths.

Although the pilot sites were free to experiment with structures, these were often variations on the Johns Hopkins directorate model in which sections of the services in each hospital were managed by a team comprising a doctor, a nurse and a manager.

During the implementation and dissemination of the Resource Management Initiative a number of key elements became clear. First, patients and the quality of service and care they received were central. Integral to this was the articulation of standards and measurements of performance against these as in medical and clinical audit. Secondly, the organizational structure was intended to be flat with power to make decisions devolved downwards. The hospital or unit was to be divided up for the purposes of management into parcels of suitable size. They were to be managed by a team including clinicians and managers. Thirdly, information systems were to be set up to provide accurate, timely and relevant information to support decisions. Fourthly, it was commonly believed that better management produced as a result of these measures would reduce inappropriate and wasteful practices and release resources.

At first, the pilot sites experimented and the rest of the NHS either ignored them or looked on with bemused interest. Later, each regional health authority set up a group of activists, coordinated and supported by the team at the Department of Health, to advise on the Resource Management Initiative and to help introduce it. These groups worked with missionary zeal and soon clinicians and managers began to realize the potential power for good contained within the initiative. Variants of a directorate structure appeared and power to make decisions gradually began to be devolved. What had started at the six pilot sites as mere smoulderings soon flared up and spread like forest fires.

Working for Patients 1989   The Prime Minister's review of the NHS in 1989 led to the development of Hospital Trusts. It was envisaged that these would have greater freedom and power devolved to them. GP fundholding, a concept derived from the North American Health Maintenance Organization model, was also introduced. Decision-making was moving closer to the patient.

A new role was defined for the district health authorities whereby they were to become purchasers of services from hospitals, including Trust Hospitals and others, which were to become known as providers.

Contracts between purchasers, including GP fundholders, and providers would define service levels and outcomes. An element of competition would be introduced and for the first time an attempt was made to define systematically the health needs of a population and to provide for these with some degree of equity.

Medical audit was firmly embedded in the report and described as 'critical analysis of the quality of medical care, including the procedures used for diagnosis and treatment, the use of resources and the resulting outcome for the patient'. For the first time this became a requirement of medical staff.

A familiar resonance can be found between some aspects of the *Working for Patients* report and Sir Roy Griffiths' vision.

Other reforms Other national initiatives since 1989 impinging on the management of health care included the shift of resources from secondary to primary care, care in the community, the introduction of multi-disciplinary clinical audit, the reduction of junior doctors' hours and the shortening of specialist training in line with the European Community.

QUALITY IN THE The need for the NHS to manage the quality of its services has been
1990S increasingly acknowledged. It was integral to the vision of the Resource Management Initiative and that of Sir Roy Griffiths and it has subsequently been developed through clinical audit and the contracting process. The trend parallels a concept first seen in what is now one of the most advanced industrialized societies in the world – Japan.

Edwards Deming (1986) first developed a concept of total quality management in Japan in 1950s. The resulting meteoric rise in the quality, attractiveness and functionality of Japanese goods and the success of its industries are now a matter of history. Having succeeded in Japan it was rediscovered in the USA where it is still a powerful movement. The case for its introduction into the NHS is vigorously made by Berwick and his colleagues. 'With it there is little to keep British health care and the NHS from being the example for the world to envy that it has been in the past' (Berwick, Enthoven and Bunker, 1992).

THE MANAGEMENT Arising out of the complex series of changes in the management of
OF CLINICAL the NHS over the last 12 years four main elements can be identified.
SERVICES

◆ A commitment to decentralizing clinical management with decisions being taken as near to the patient level as possible.
◆ Decentralized clinical management being carried out by multi-disciplinary team as the preferred approach.
◆ The management of quality to become part of NHS culture.
◆ Timely, relevant and accurate information required to support decision-making.

ORGANIZATIONAL STRUCTURE OF AN ACUTE PROVIDER UNIT

There are three levels of management which must work together to manage the service effectively: the Trust Board, the Trust Management Group and the directorate teams. It is vital that all three have clearly defined roles, coordinate well and have a good understanding of clinical management.

The Trust Board

The Trust Board is made up of a chairperson appointed by the Secretary of State and an equal number of executive and non-executive directors up to five of each. The executive members must include the chief executive, the finance officer, and the nursing and medical directors. The Trust Board is responsible for 'determining the overall policies of the trust, monitoring the execution of the agreed policies and maintaining financial viability of the trust' (*NHS Trusts: A Working Guide*, 1991).

The Trust Management Group

The Trust Management Group is responsible, in conjunction with the Trust Board, for strategic planning and acts as the operational decision-making body carrying out the policies of the Trust Board.

The membership of the Trust Management Group is variable but usually includes the executive directors of the Trust Board together with agreed clinical and support team leaders. Where there are fewer directorates all the clinical directors may well sit on the Board; where a larger number of directorates exist some form of clustering and representation is common.

The Directorate Management Team

The directorate management team is emerging as the fundamental, multidisciplinary operational unit which manages clinical services. The goal of the directorate is to identify explicitly the range of financial and other resources available to provide patient care, and to ensure that these resources are used to the greatest effect for the benefit of patients.

Each directorate is usually responsible for a defined part of a Trust's services; how these services are grouped varies widely as does the number and size of directorates. In a recent survey the budget for each team was between 2 million and 4 million pounds. First-wave Trusts, where the management structures have matured, often have larger directorates – 12% of directorates in first-wave Trusts hold budgets over 8.5 million pounds (British Association of Medical Managers *et al.*, 1993).

The Acute Unit Directorate Model

This is often a variant of the directorate structure derived from Johns Hopkins Hospital in Baltimore. There is usually a consultant as clinical director together with a nurse and a business manager in support.

Clinical work limits the amount of time the clinical director can devote to management and this often dictates the distribution of work amongst the team. However, the business manager (or directorate general manager) usually has responsibility for finance, information and the business elements of management. The nurse is usually responsible for nursing and nurse staff management as well as quality management. The director usually has overall responsibility for the directorate with a particular role in leadership, representing the directorate, liaising with medical colleagues within the directorate and the development of a business plan. A more complete list of these functions is included later in this chapter.

In larger directorates with large budgets a whole-time finance officer and perhaps a part-time personnel officer may well be included in the team. Smaller directorates usually share these services.

The widely varying services encompassed within community Trusts and their widespread geographical distribution have led to many different models of clinical management to meet their specific needs. Management may well be based on local needs and the director may not be a doctor (British Association of Medical Managers *et al.*, 1993).

KEY ROLES FOR DOCTORS

The Medical Director of the Trust Board

The doctor occupying this post is usually appointed by the chief executive after wide soundings amongst his or her colleagues. The person concerned must be respected by, and acceptable to, both the Trust Board and the body of doctors. The medical director is on the Trust Board to provide a strategic medical overview.

Job descriptions often include specific requirements such as the provision of advice on clinical policies, the monitoring of medical performance, the management of the Trust's clinical audit, the medical disciplinary matters and the reduction of junior doctors' hours. In only 13% of Trusts in a recent survey were the clinical directors responsible to the medical director (British Association of Medical Managers *et al.*, 1993). This is reducing still further and is now 5% (British Association of Medical Managers Survey 1994, interim results. Personal communication).

The Clinical Director

Doctors occupying these posts are usually appointed by the chief executive after ensuring acceptability to the consultant body. Seventy-five per cent of clinical directors were doctors and 65% were responsible to the chief executive (British Association of Medical Managers *et al.*, 1993).

In practice the majority of clinical directors questioned spent between two and four sessions per week on their directorate duties, most spending three sessions (British Association of Medical Managers *et al.*, 1993; Wraith and Casey, 1992).

The functions of the Clinical Director are listed in Box 1.1.

Box 1.1
Functions of the
clinical director

◆ Promoting a sense of directorate identity and helping to develop the direction, pace and culture of the directorate in collaboration with others.

◆ Developing leadership qualities in themselves and others.

◆ Encouraging a team spirit within the directorate.

◆ Representing the directorate at Trust management level.

◆ Developing the directorate business plan and monitoring performance against it.

◆ Leading on quality standards including clinical audit in the directorate.

◆ The overall management of staff – this is often delegated to others.

◆ Promoting communication within the directorate.

The Chief Executive Officer

Very few doctors aspire to occupy this post as yet. The national expectations are that the position is full time which would mean giving up clinical practice. A significant amount of management experience in many roles together with additional formal management training would normally be required.

THE CONSEQUENCES OF HOLDING MANAGEMENT POSTS

All those working in hospital medicine have been frustrated over the years by the creaking machinery of the NHS. Taking up a management post is a golden opportunity to listen to the views of many people and to bring them together into a coherent plan for change. By quite small changes significant benefits for patients and staff can often accrue.

However, management posts are demanding, not least in terms of time. The responsibilities of the post and its demands must be recognized and adequate support put in place to make the role both possible and successful. On the positive side, human beings delight in learning new skills and acquiring those involved in management is no exception.

Relationships with colleagues can be significantly changed. If the approach of the director is to be dictatorial the change may well be for the worst. If by 'director' we mean a person who helps with his or her colleagues to establish a direction for the team by listening to colleagues' aspirations then the changes in the relationships are likely to be for the better.

Relationships with managers are refreshing in that their viewpoints will often be quite different from those of clinicians and useful dialogue can result.

CAREER DEVELOPMENT FOR CLINICAL MANAGERS

For most doctors the post of clinical director will be as far as they wish to go in management. It is quite possible after four years or so to revert to full-time clinical practice although some sessions may have been lost over that time. For those who wish to go on to become medical directors being a clinical director is a very useful apprenticeship.

Medical directors occupy a powerful position on the Trust Board and they are in a good position to influence Trust policy. Usually it requires more than the three sessions common for clinical directors; five or six sessions are more likely. To occupy such a post is a clear career change. The way back into full-time clinical practice is correspondingly difficult but possible with some planning.

For those who aspire to become a chief executive the course is longer and the post is certainly full time. It is unlikely that any such person would either want, or be able, to return to clinical practice. Hitherto, only a small number of doctors have trodden this path. Nevertheless, their training as doctors potentially gives them the benefit of enormous insight. Who better than a doctor to be at the table when difficult decisions are being made which impinge upon patients and who could be better placed to come up with imaginative solutions and enthuse their colleagues? More of these posts will probably be occupied by doctors in the future as the medical profession grasps at the opportunities in management.

For doctors to occupy any of these roles training and support is necessary although often lacking. A network of like-minded colleagues is helpful. The British Association of Medical Managers was set up in 1991 especially to meet these needs. It is dedicated to the promotion of quality health care by improving and supporting the contribution of doctors in management.

Space prevents full discussion of the many skills required in order to be a good clinical manager but many of these are addressed in the following chapters.

THE WAY FORWARD

Although the recent changes in the NHS outlined earlier in the chapter have thrust into doctors' hands a golden opportunity it is one that we can easily lose by default. However, there are only two choices: we either lead or we are led. To be led would not only be humiliating for the medical profession but also deprive the NHS of an invaluable source of energy and creativity. On the other hand, to pick up the torch and run with it and to lead gives us the opportunity to provide the best quality of patient care within whatever resources we have. Surely, that is at the heart of our ideals as doctors. In addition, it is often exciting and rewarding to do so.

SUMMARY

- In 1983 Roy Griffiths investigated the health service and made recommendations for changing its management structure.
- The influence of the Griffiths report has been enormous and has led to managerial decisions being made much closer to the patient level.
- The Resource Management Initiative was an important catalyst for change along the lines recommended by Griffiths.
- The Clinical Directorate structure enables a team made up of doctors and other healthcare workers together with managers to use resources to the best advantage.
- We are presented with a golden opportunity to influence the care of patients and shape the future health service.

USEFUL ADDRESS   The British Association of Medical Managers,
Barnes Hospital,
Kingsway,
Cheadle,
Cheshire,
SK8 2NY

FURTHER READING

- British Association of Medical Managers, British Medical Association, Institute of Health Services Management, Royal College of Nursing (1993), *Managing Clinical Services, A consensus statement of principles for effective clinical management*, IHSM, London.

This statement was based on research carried out in a variety of provider settings throughout the country, including community settings. It firmly supports the directorate structure as the main driving unit for the new devolved managerial structure in the NHS. Produced by a working party containing members of The British Association of Medical Managers, The British Medical Association, The Institute of Health Service Management and The Royal College of Nursing.

- Ham, D. and Hunter, D.J. (1988), *Managing Clinical Activity in the NHS*, Kings Fund Institute, London.

A useful academic view on the structural problems in the NHS. Describes the types of conflict that occur between clinical and managerial staff.

> ◆ Institute of Health Services Management (1990), *Models of Clinical Management*, IHSM, London.
>
> This is a pioneering work setting out the variety of models of clinical management in the early days. It was the basis for most further studies in these areas.
>
> ◆ Wraith, M. and Casey, A. (1992), *Implementing Clinically Based Management – Getting Organisational Change Underway, A handbook for doctors, nurses and other hospital managers*. Wraith Casey, Worcester.
>
> This is a short, very readable and excellent account about implementing clinically based management. It was written by two management consultants with wide experience of the NHS and implementing management change.

REFERENCES

Berwick D.M., Enthoven, A. and Bunker, J.P. (1992a), Quality Management in the NHS: The doctor's role – I. *British Medical Journal* **304**: 235.

Berwick, D.M., Enthoven, A. and Bunker, J.P. (1992b), Quality Management in the NHS: The doctor's role – II. *British Medical Journal* **304**: 304.

British Association of Medical Managers, British Medical Association, Institute of Health Services Management, Royal College of Nursing (1993), *Managing Clinical Services*. London: IHSM.

Deming, W.E. (1986), *Out of the Crisis*. Cambridge University Press.

Department of Health (1989), *Working For Patients*. London: HMSO.

Griffiths, R. (1983), *NHS Management Inquiry for Department of Health and Social Security*.

Griffiths, R. (1992), *Who cares? – Management and the caring services. Journal of the Royal Society of Medicine* **85**: 663.

Griffiths, R. (1994), Introduction to general management. In: Burrows, M., Dyson, R., Jackson, P. and Saxton, H. (Eds). *Management For Hospital Doctors*, p. 41. Oxford: Butterworth-Heinemann.

Health Notice 1986, No. 34. Heywood, Lancs: DSS Distribution Centre.

NHS Trusts: A Working Guide (1991), London: HMSO.

Wraith, M. and Casey, A. (1992), *Implementing Clinically Based Management – Getting Organisational Change Underway. A Handbook for Doctors, Nurses and other Hospital Managers*. Worcester: Wraith Casey.

Yates, J. (1987), *Why Are We Waiting? An Analysis of Hospital Waiting Lists*. Oxford University Press.

STATUTORY AND LEGAL RESPONSIBILITIES OF THE DOCTOR IN MANAGEMENT

CHAPTER 2

Glenn Douglas and Richard Long

OBJECTIVES

- ◆ To outline the key legal issues of which doctors in management should be aware.
- ◆ To identify the pitfalls and problems open to the unwary.
- ◆ To provide guidelines on how to avoid them.

INTRODUCTION

This chapter provides a comprehensive outline of certain key legal issues of which clinical directors and other doctors in management should be aware. In particular these are:

- ◆ The management of risk and litigation.
- ◆ Employment law.
- ◆ Business law, particularly relating to contracts.
- ◆ Public accountability.

European Community law, where it can be distinguished, will be dealt with under each subject heading.

This chapter is set in the context of the trend towards decentralization of management responsibilities to clinical directors by Trusts. As Trusts move towards structures and commercial disciplines more resembling the private sector, clinical managers will have to make more 'business' decisions. Like private sector managers, they will not be lawyers, but they will find a basic knowledge of the law an important aid to decision-making.

THE MANAGEMENT OF RISK AND LITIGATION

Why is this important?

By its very nature, some activities of a clinical directorate are risky. This is not necessarily a bad thing but it is important that those who take risks do so from an informed position. There is the potential to lose a lot of money if proper risk management is not undertaken.

Clinical negligence

The main area of risk to a Trust is clinical negligence. The costs of settling litigation for clinical negligence are escalating at an alarming rate. Although not reaching levels seen in the United States, they are already cutting into NHS resources (and indirectly clinical directorate budgets), thus affecting the level and quality of patient care.

The legal basis for clinical negligence is through the legal principle of tort, which allows individuals to sue the Trust for committing a 'wrong', in this case negligence. Several hurdles must be overcome for a claim to be successful (Box 2.1).

Box 2.1
Tort

Duty:	the defendant must be under a duty to exercise reasonable skill and care.
Breach:	he must have failed to do so.
Damage:	the patient must have suffered loss or damage.
Causation:	as a result of that failure.

The legal duty of a medical practitioner to exercise reasonable skill and care in treating a patient or client was established in Pippin v. Sterrad, 1822. In Bolam v. Friern Hospital Management Committee, 1957, it was found that 'a doctor is not guilty of negligence if he has acted in accordance with a practice accepted as proper by a responsible body of medical men skilled in that particular art ... a doctor is not negligent if he is acting in accordance with such a practice, merely because there is a body of opinion that takes a contrary view'. This is often known as the Bolam Test. However, it has since been confirmed in subsequent medico-legal cases that the court is the final arbiter of a professional standard.

Other forms of risk

Clinical negligence is only one, if very expensive, risk to be avoided; many others will impinge on the working of a clinical directorate. A list of potential areas needing attention are shown in Figure 2.1.

Risk management should be clearly seen to be at the centre of the directorate's activities and the inherent risks. This sounds very daunting but in practice most risk management issues are really

Figure 2.1
Risk management at the centre of a directorate's operations

DIRECTORATE

Health and safety · Security · Fire · Control of infection · Communication · Staffing · Resuscitation · RISK · Documentation · Consent · Competence · Delay in treatment · Provision of goods and services · Waste · Buildings, plant and equipment

OPERATIONS

common sense. It does not even have to cost money: most risks can be managed effectively without the need for expensive renovations or new systems.

Risk management in practice

There are four stages to putting risk management into practice:

1. *Risk identification*: Identifying what could go wrong, how it could happen and what the effect would be.
2. *Risk analysis*: Taking the identified risk and estimating the likely frequency, cost and severity.
3. *Risk control*: Considering how the risks can be eliminated, avoided, made less likely or less costly.
4. *Risk funding*: Considering what needs to be insured (transferring risk) or shared with an 'excess'. (An excess is the element of risk which is self insured, an example is in car insurance where you agree to pay the first £100 of any claim). Alternatively, the risk may be kept within the organization, which is known as self insurance. The option of insurance currently only applies to non-clinical negligence risks for which Trusts are responsible.

What do I do as a clinical director?

It can seem an intimidating task to grasp the full implications of risk management. However, you should not be alone. Most, if not all, Trusts will have some form of risk management strategy. Consult any documentation available or, preferably, be involved in the process of constructing such documentation. Relevant specialist skills are usually available within the Trust such as security, health and safety, building, engineering and microbiology. It may be a good idea to nominate someone from your directorate to be responsible for risk management. Many Trusts now employ a risk manager. Find out who they are and use their services.

Risk management:
Concluding
comments

Risk management is important for everyone in the organization. In essence it is common sense and deserves consideration from you, both as a clinician and as a manager. Take stock of the directorate you work in and identify the risks that appear to you. Then, think how to minimize them and you are on your way.

BUSINESS LAW

Corporate identity

NHS Trusts are recognized by the law as legal 'persons' having the ability to contract with other 'persons' and to sue and be sued. However, they are not regulated by the Companies Acts 1985–1989, but are each created by regulations under the National Health Service and Community Care Act 1990, referred to as the 1990 Act in this chapter. It would have been much simpler and clearer if they had been conventional companies regulated by the Companies Acts. Company law is well established and codified. It is not necessary for limited companies to have shares and be profit making. A special category of these companies, 'companies limited by guarantee' have neither, and this format is commonly used by registered charities.

The many grey areas in NHS Trust (company) law are being filled by the rapidly accumulating body of guidance issued by the NHS Executive. However, for most purposes relevant to clinical managers, NHS Trusts behave like conventional companies.

Principles of law

The three principal areas of law in which companies may find themselves entangled are:

◆ *Tort*. The common law right of persons and companies to sue the Trust for committing one of several legally defined 'wrongs', of which by far the most important is negligence. It is upon this tort that virtually all clinical negligence claims are based (see above).

◆ *Statute*. This heading includes the many and diverse Acts and regulations which govern parts of clinical practice as well as management. Breach of any of them may give rise to criminal liability. These range from the 1961 Factories Act, the 1963 Offices Shops and Railway Premises Act, the 1969 Employers Liability (Defective Equipment) Act, the 1993 Radioactive Substances Act through to the obscure 1952 Hypnotism Act. These Acts and regulations represent large and small minefields into which the unwary can easily stray. The secret to avoiding them is to ensure that any plans or new initiatives are widely circulated to professionals (such as surveyors and accountants) working in your Trust in the hope that they may spot any possible problems and seek specialist legal advice. Doctors and those in other clinical disciplines will usually be the best source of information on clinical regulations. If you have an in-house lawyer working in your Trust you have a head start.

♦ *Contract.* Contract is one of the areas of law in which a little learning, far from being dangerous, will be repaid many times. All clinical directors and business managers should understand the basic principles involved.

Contract law   All business transactions are based on contracts. This term applies to any legally enforceable agreement between two or more parties, whether or not it is in writing. There is a commonly held belief, in business as well as in the NHS, that a verbal agreement or an exchange of letters amounts to no more than a negotiable understanding, rendered into something enforceable only after the intercession of two firms of solicitors, numerous pages of text ('the legal stuff'), a quantity of non-standard size high quality paper and the application of a closely guarded metal seal to a red plastic wafer. In fact none of these steps are necessary to the formation of a legally binding contract. Only those listed in Box 2.2 are required.

Box 2.2
Requirements for a
legally binding contract

> ♦ *An offer* on certain (defined) terms (to provide goods or services or to pay for them if provided).
>
> ♦ *Acceptance* of the offer (which must be unconditional) (the offer and acceptance together comprise agreement).
>
> ♦ *Consideration* (that is, payment which must not pre-date the agreement).
>
> ♦ *An intention to create legal relations* (which is presumed between commercial parties).

It follows that there are numerous traps for the unwary: it is an easy matter to create a contract when you do not intend to, or fail to create a contract when you wanted to. Remember that a contract need not be in writing. If your business manager orders a piece of equipment from a supplier and they agree to supply, a contract is formed. Equally, if you fail to set out unambiguous terms there may be no contract, or the terms which are ambiguous may be unenforceable. An interesting rule, which can work both ways, is that ambiguous terms are construed against whoever drafted them. This is often useful when you are looking for ways to avoid unpleasant terms which you had not bothered to read before entering into a contract with a supplier.

It must be clear who are the parties to a contract. They must be the parties who will perform the obligations in the contract. For instance if the supplier is US Copiers Limited, it is no use the contract stating that another company, not a party to the contract, will maintain the copier free of charge. That company must also be a party to the contract.

If you wish to enforce the terms of a contract against a party to it, it must be signed by that party. For this reason it is usual for there to be two copies of every contract, signed by both (or all) parties, each keeping a copy.

It is vital to keep a copy of a contract and, if it refers to published terms not contained in the contract itself, to ensure that you have a copy of these terms (preferably before you sign the contract).

Contracts must be signed by people having actual or ostensible authority to do so. It is safest when dealing with companies to insist that a director of the company signs. It is good practice for your own organization to insist on the same procedure.

The use of the words 'subject to contract' is a useful convention to enable you to negotiate the outline of a contract in correspondence without being held prematurely to an initial proposal before you are completely happy with all the terms. The use of these words at the head of any letter will enable you to use it in negotiations.

One area where the above common law rules do not apply is in property (land and buildings). Property law is a large and complex branch of commercial law. One important difference is that property contracts do have to be in writing. Another is that far reaching and expensive rights can easily be created unintentionally. For instance, any company or business partnership (for example, a GP practice) which is allowed to occupy NHS premises in return for payment of any kind is likely to acquire security of tenure. While it may be possible to bring pressure, perhaps through the local Family Health Service Authority (FHSA), to undo this, it will, at least, be a headache.

NHS contracts   The 1990 Act defines an NHS contract (in section 4.1) as 'an arrangement under which one health service body ("the Acquirer") arranges for the provision to it by another health service body ("the Provider") of goods or services which it reasonably requires for the provision of its functions'. It goes on to define 'health service body' predictably, except that non-fundholding GP practices are not included. The section then states:

> *Whether or not an arrangement which constitutes an NHS contract would, apart from this sub-section, be a contract in law, it shall not be regarded for any purpose as giving rise to contractual rights or*

liabilities, but if any dispute arises with respect to such an arrangement, either party may refer the matter to the Secretary of State for determination.

In practice it seems that the NHS does not intend taxpayers' money to be spent by Trusts and health authorities on lawyers and courts, but believes that the NHS Executive will be able to arbitrate on contentious matters more cheaply and more efficiently. This may be so. However, caution should be exercised. The courts do not like to have their functions limited in this way and have already decided that contracts, if they appear to be legally enforceable, may be taken to court, even though they are between two health service bodies. It seems likely that the annual contracts between providers and purchasers, and service level agreements between Trusts, will continue to enjoy this exemption. However, advice should be sought where there is any doubt.

This does not mean that the basic rules of contract law can be ignored with NHS contracts. Although it is unclear what criteria the NHS Executive will use to resolve disputes, it seems likely, in the absence of further clarification, that it will use rules approximating to the law of contract. It may, however, modify the law of contract by using its discretion to exclude contract terms it considers unreasonable.

Contract: Key points
Box 2.3 lists the key points that will help you through the contract minefield.

Box 2.3
Contract: key points

♦ Be clear about who are the parties to a contract.

♦ Be sure the terms are unambiguous and not left 'to be agreed'.

♦ Be clear about what a contract is and when one comes into existence.

♦ If you are presented with a contract to sign, read it and argue any terms with which you are unhappy.

♦ If in doubt, but only when you have employed common sense to its full, get legal advice.

EMPLOYMENT LAW   The NHS is now said to be, following the demise of the Soviet Army, the largest employer in Europe. Most NHS Trusts employ between 1000 and 5000 employees and spend the majority of their budget on pay. Proper management of staff and control of this element of the budget is therefore an important part of a clinical manager's responsibilities. Most Trust directors of human resources will be well trained in employment law and clinical managers should be able to rely on them for good advice. However, a basic understanding of employment law will be an advantage.

The aim of this part of the chapter is to explain the difference between employees and the self-employed, to outline the various statutory and other legal rights of employees and to put these points in the context of NHS employment.

Employee versus self-employed   It is important to distinguish between the two. Employers have onerous liabilities towards their employees, but relatively few towards anyone who is self-employed. The treatment of pay and tax for the two groups is very different. Most staff of an NHS Trust will be employees.

Advice should be taken over the status of consultants, whose contracts of employment may now differ between Trusts. However, they are likely to be employees in law. In contrast, GPs are self-employed, contracting independently and through partnerships with the NHS. At present it is rare for NHS Trusts to use self-employed staff.

The basis of the relationship between an employer and employee is the contract of employment. This has traditionally been regulated by the detailed terms negotiated at the Whitley Council, but looks set to change. However, certain things are assumed or implied in any contract of employment, whether or not they are stated expressly, such as the duty of the employer to pay the employee and provide work.

Express terms   Anything else must be dealt with in the written contract of employment. By law the employer must give the employee a written statement of the main contract terms not later than 13 weeks after commencement of employment.

Rights of the employee during employment   The main obligation of both employer and employee during employment is not to break the terms of the contract. So, in practice in the NHS, if an employee is contracted to do a certain job during specified hours with so much holiday and so much guaranteed time off for training, the employer may not unilaterally change these aspects. If changes are made to the detriment of the employee he or she may be entitled to resign and claim constructive dismissal. This may lead to proceedings in the Industrial Tribunal, which will be discussed later. Even as Trusts change their conditions of employment, usually to make them more flexible, the basic principle will always hold: you may not unilaterally change an employee's conditions of employment. To do so is a breach of contract, and the employee will be entitled to compensation for whatever loss he or she has suffered.

Although there are ways of terminating the employment of someone who is not working satisfactorily, the required procedure is so fraught with difficulty that the advice of your director of human resources and/or a specialist employment lawyer is essential.

The Protection of Employment Act 1975 and The Employment Protection (Consolidation) Act 1978

If you get it wrong, and terminate someone's employment when you should not have, the case may very well end up in an Industrial Tribunal. The main exception to this is if a full-time employee has worked in the NHS for less than two years. In this case he or she will have no recourse to the Tribunal. Special rules apply to part-time employees.

Every employee has the right not to be unfairly dismissed. Some classes of employees are excluded, but this is unlikely to apply to employees of an NHS Trust. Any dismissal will be presumed unfair unless the employer can show that it was for:

♦ Capability (lack of skill/aptitude/health to do the job).
♦ Conduct (justifying dismissal).
♦ Redundancy (in which case you have to pay redundancy).
♦ To avoid breaking the law.
♦ Some other substantial reason of a kind such as to justify the dismissal of an employee holding the position which that employee held.

Even then the Tribunal must decide whether the dismissal was fair or unfair in the context of the reason given by the employer and whether the employer acted reasonably in treating that reason as a sufficient reason for dismissal.

Redundancy

Employers may deliberately make employees redundant and accept the cost, which will be less than payment for unfair dismissal. However, care needs to be taken that someone is not selected for redundancy on unfair grounds. If so, they may qualify for the higher payment for unfair dismissal.

You can dismiss an employee for redundancy if

♦ the employer has ceased or intends to cease to carry on the business for the purposes for which the employee was employed, or in the place where the employee was so employed;
   or
♦ the requirement for employees to carry out work of a particular kind or in the place where they were so employed has ceased or diminished or is expected to.

There are a number of other provisions; for instance the employer may be able to offer alternative employment and, if unreasonably refused, the employee may lose his or her rights to redundancy payment. Employers must consult with trade unions where redundancies are proposed and, in case of large-scale redundancies, must inform the Secretary of State.

One important limitation is that, in order to exercise his/her redundancy rights, an employee must complain to an Industrial Tribunal within three months of termination. This time limit is applied strictly. The Tribunal may award reinstatement/re-engagement or compensation, calculated on a formula.

Statutory maternity rights   A pregnant woman has five statutory rights. The provisions are very detailed:

♦ Time off for antenatal care.
♦ A right not to be unfairly dismissed for any reason connected with pregnancy.
♦ A right to return to work.
♦ A right to statutory maternity pay.
♦ A right not to be discriminated against on the ground of her sex.

Transfer of a business   A very topical subject in business and the NHS is the question of employees' rights following the transfer of an undertaking. Until recently the public sector was exempt from these provisions, which originally came about following a European directive on the subject. Following cases in the European courts under the same directive, the public sector is now no longer exempt from the Transfer of Undertakings (Protection of Employment) Regulations 1981. The most important provisions are:

♦ A dismissal for a reason connected with the transfer of an undertaking is prima facie unfair and the employee may be able to claim against both the transferor and/or transferee business. This now applies to dismissals taking place before, after or at the time of the transfer.
♦ Employees transferring with a business take with themselves all accrued rights.

This has two significant applications in the NHS:

♦ All employees who transferred into Trusts have rights, including length of service etc., as if they had continued to work for the same employer.
♦ If an NHS Trust attempts to sub-contract or market test a service currently provided in-house, both it and any new contractor may be landed with claims from the employee who loses their job. This has important and obvious implications for the feasibility of market testing. On the other hand, if a Trust merely transfers a contract for services from one sub-contractor to another, the Trust cannot be liable in this way. This is, depending on your point of view, strong grounds either for sub-contracting everything at the first opportunity or never sub-contracting anything if you can help it. It is certainly questionable whether

market testing of in-house service departments against external contractors can, in the light of these regulations, ever be a realistic exercise.

PUBLIC ACCOUNTABILITY

Introduction

The probity of government organizations has been a matter of considerable public debate for some time. It is a long standing principle that the NHS, as a public body, should be seen to be impartial and honest. The legal jurisdiction for this is the Prevention of Corruption Acts 1906 and 1916, which deem it an offence for an employee corruptly to accept any inducement or reward for doing, or refraining from doing, anything in his or her official capacity, or corruptly showing favour, or disfavour, in the handling of contracts. A breach of the provisions of these Acts renders employees liable to prosecution and may also lead to loss of their employment and superannuation rights.

As a directorate manager, the clinical director is responsible for the spending of large sums of money and therefore has to be clear what can or cannot be done.

Issues

Although the preceding points may seem over-prescriptive, particularly to doctors, most of what has been described is common sense. The NHS Executive general guidelines identify principles of conduct. These are set out in Box 2.4.

Box 2.4
Principles of conduct for NHS staff

NHS staff are expected to:

♦ Ensure that the interests of patients remain paramount at all times.

♦ Be impartial and honest in the conduct of their official business.

♦ Use the public funds entrusted to them to the best advantage of the service, always ensuring value for money.

It is also the responsibility of staff to ensure that they do not:

♦ Abuse their official position for personal gain or to benefit their family or friends.

Source: Standards of Business Conduct for NHS Staff, January 1993

♦ Seek to advantage or further private business or other interests, in the course of their official duties.

Returning to the common sense theme, a good indicator of whether something is acceptable or not is to consider what the reaction would be if the press knew about it. If it passes this test then it will probably be acceptable. However, to protect yourself, if you are in any doubt discuss it with your chief executive, and confirm it in writing.

Declaration of interests   Where any employee or a close relative has a significant financial interest in a business which may compete for an NHS contract, they should declare such an interest and disbar themselves from any selection procedure. The clinical director should keep a directorate register of interests in line with the Trust's policy. Remember, ultimately it is in the best interests of the staff concerned to ensure such a declaration is made.

Hospitality   You should treat with caution all offers of hospitality wherever any suggestion can arise of improper influence. Particular care is required where hospitality is offered by a person or body having or seeking business with the Trust, particularly where the offer is to you as an individual. It should only be accepted where it is on a scale appropriate to the circumstances, reasonably incidental to the occasion and where it is apparent no cause could reasonably arise for adverse criticism about accepting it. Thus a working lunch to a modest standard, a drink following a site inspection or hospitality extended by another non-commercial body would all, on an appropriate scale, be acceptable. An offer of a holiday, an evening out or any significant personal benefit would not.

Public accountability: Concluding comments   As part of the public sector, the standard of integrity demanded of the Trust's employees is exceptionally high. As in so many other areas common sense is needed and the simple rule to follow is *'if in doubt – don't'*. In this way you will protect yourself against future accusations of impropriety.

Most professional bodies, and the General Medical Council (GMC) is no exception, require members to adhere to professional standards. Part 2, paragraph 57 of the GMC's *Professional Conduct and Discipline* (1993) sets out the principles of declaring interests and ensuring that you are protected against any accusations. This is reproduced below:

> *Doctors, like lay members or officers of any health authority, have a duty to declare an interest before participating in discussions which could lead to the purchase by a public authority of goods or services in which they, or a member of their immediate family, have a direct or indirect pecuniary interest. Non disclosure of such information may, under certain circumstances, amount to serious professional misconduct.*

CONCLUSION   This chapter has identified a number of key statutory and legal areas which impinge on the operation of a clinical directorate or the activities of the individual doctor in management. Despite the legalistic side to these issues a recurrent theme is that of common sense when dealing with these issues. No one expects the doctor in management to be a lawyer but in this case a little knowledge can be a good thing, as long as it is tempered by a willingness to ask for help.

SUMMARY

> The key points of this chapter can be summarized as follows:
>
> ♦ Proper risk management is essential to avoid unnecessary cost and detrimental health care.
> ♦ The main area of risk is through clinical negligence.
> ♦ Risk management covers all the activities of a clinical directorate.
> ♦ NHS Trusts in most cases behave like conventional companies.
> ♦ Always read any contract and only sign if you agree with it all. If in doubt and you have employed common sense to the full, get advice.
> ♦ You should have a basic understanding of employment law.
> ♦ The issues surrounding public accountability are really about applying common sense judgements to situations.

STATUTES REFERRED TO
The Companies Act 1985
The Companies Act 1989
The National Health Service and Community Care Act 1990
The Factories Act 1961
The Offices Shops and Railway Premises Act 1963
The Employers Liability (Defective Equipment) Act 1969
The Hypnotism Act 1952
The Radioactive Substances Act 1993
The Protection of Employment Act 1975
The Employment Protection (Consolidation) Act 1978
The Prevention of Corruption Acts 1906; 1916

LIST OF REGULATIONS
The Transfer of Undertakings (Protection of Employment) Regulations 1981
General Medical Council: *Professional Conduct and Discipline* Part 2: Dishonesty: Improper Financial Transactions, Paragraph 57, 1993

FURTHER READING

♦ Finch, J. (1994) *Speller's Law Relating to Hospitals*, 7th edn, Chapman & Hall Medical, London.

A very good, if long, relevant text as a basis for law as it affects the NHS.

♦ NHS Management Executive (1993), *Risk Management in the NHS*.

This gives a very comprehensive analysis of risk management and guides the reader to specific and relevant examples.

♦ NHS Management Executive (1993), *Standards of Business Conduct for NHS Staff*, HSG(93)5.

An essential document for any clinician or manager in the NHS to have read. Particularly valuable as it shows how seemingly innocent actions can be perceived in the outside world.

CHAPTER 3

MANAGING FINANCE

Glenn Douglas

OBJECTIVES

◆ To explore the major issues in NHS finance.

◆ To show the relevance of these issues to the operation of a clinical directorate.

◆ To provide practical guidelines on how the clinician in management can deal with these issues.

INTRODUCTION

Finance is a major area for doctors in management to understand. Finance staff, like all professionals, are prone to shroud the key knowledge needed with jargon.

This chapter sets out to highlight the current issues in health finance and to give clinicians in management an understanding of the financial regime in which they operate.

In order to achieve these objectives, this chapter addresses a number of important financial points:

◆ The NHS Trust financial regime.
◆ Costing and pricing (to be read in conjunction with the chapter on contracting).
◆ Budgets and budgetary information.
◆ Capital charges.
◆ Investment decisions.
◆ Treasury management.
◆ Value for money.

The chapter then concludes with some hints on how to use and manage your finance manager.

NHS TRUST FINANCIAL REGIME

A Trust operates in much the same way as a business. Income is derived from selling services, mainly patient care, to purchasers of health care, namely health authorities, commissioning agencies or GP fundholders. Expenditure is then matched to expected income and budgets derived from them.

Figure 3.1
The three
card trick

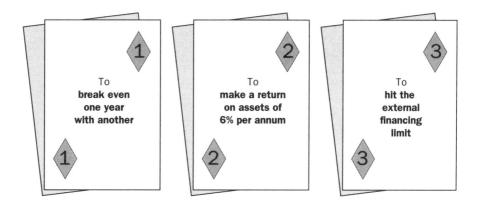

A Trust is closely monitored by the National Health Service Executive (NHSE) who determine three key financial targets. This can be viewed as a three card trick, as shown in Figure 3.1.

The trick can be explained as

◆ Breaking even means that the Trust must not lose money in any financial year.

◆ Making a 6% return on assets; this is linked with breaking even as half the worth of the Trust is loaned by the government as interest bearing debt at currently 6.5% interest and half by public dividend capital at 5.5% interest, which together equate to a 6% return. Although the precise interest rate of each element is variable, the sum should always equate to 6%.

◆ The external financing limit (EFL) is the means used by the NHSE for controlling the amount spent on capital. The way this is used to control capital expenditure is that by hitting your target EFL it only allows you to spend up to your agreed capital expenditure programme. Any spending in excess of this would mean you would not achieve one part of the trick.

Overall the NHSE retains very strict controls over the finances of the notionally 'independent' Trusts.

COSTING AND
PRICING

Introduction

In the workings of the internal market one of the most important aspects of finance to understand is costing and pricing and the relationship between the two.

Failure to achieve accurate pricing could mean the directorate or Trust having severe financial difficulties. The process is often seen as a finance department issue. It is not. It is vitally important that clinical staff within directorates, together with business managers, play an active role in pricing services. After all that is where the clinical activities are carried out. The key to successful pricing is a sound knowledge of costs. The various dimensions of costing, together with its uses and attributes, are shown in Figure 3.2.

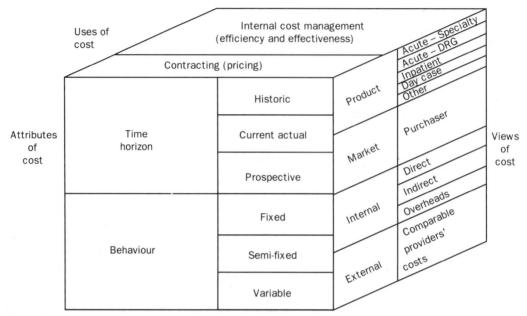

Figure 3.2
Specialty and procedure pricing – your requirements

Fundamental There are three fundamental principles on which pricing in the
principles NHS is based, listed in Box 3.1.

Box 3.1
Pricing: fundamental
principles

♦ Prices should be based on costs.

♦ Costs should be arrived at on a full cost basis.

♦ There should be no planned cross subsidization between
contracts.

This last point is important because it can put the Trust at a
disadvantage when competing with the private sector which can
price low in order to attract new business. At the time of writing,
it seems likely that this rule will be relaxed to enable fairer
competition.

Process of costing It can be seen that the key to pricing is through costing. Figure 3.3
shows the two ways to achieve individual costs for procedures or
groups of procedures. These are the top down approach and the
bottom up approach.

The top down approach is where the total costs of a Trust are
allocated or apportioned *down* to specialties or even procedures.
The bottom up approach builds *up* the total costs of a directorate

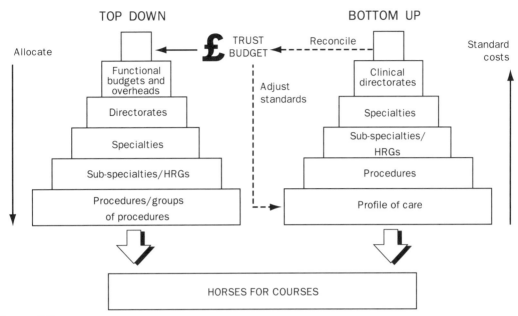

Figure 3.3
Specialty and procedure pricing – costing and pricing approaches

by identifying the costs of each activity, using profiles of care for each procedure. This builds the total cost for the service.

It is imperative, when attempting the bottom up method, that all costs are covered. To do this a reconciliation must occur with total costs, to avoid missing hidden elements of cost overheads.

In practice, a combination of both methods is usually appropriate for costing your services. It may be that you want to highlight high cost procedures. Additionally some form of banding similar cost procedures may make the process less arduous.

Understanding cost behaviour To understand the issues of costing fully, it is important to look at the different types of cost and how each of them behaves. This will help the clinician to unravel the finance terminology and directly influence costing and pricing in the Trust.

♦ *Direct costs* – costs which can be directly attributed to the particular activity or output being measured (cost centre or product).
♦ *Indirect costs* – cannot be attributed directly to a particular cost centre but is shared over a number of them.
♦ *Overhead costs* – costs of support services which contribute to the general running of a hospital but cannot be directly related to the volume or quantity of service provided in individual wards or departments.
♦ *Fixed costs* – costs which are unaffected by in-year activity charges.

◆ *Semi-fixed costs* – also referred to as step costs. These are only fixed for a given range of activity but, beyond this, may increase or decrease as activity varies.

◆ *Variable costs* – tend to vary with the level of activity.

When looking at the costs of your particular service, it is important to know how they have been calculated and on what basis. This is particularly useful when deciding how to price for additional activity.

Marginal costs　Although one of the key principles on which pricing is based is that they should be based on full costs, it is possible to price at a level which covers only the additional cost of providing the additional activity. However, this only applies to the pricing of additional capacity in the short term. Such contracts would be tenable only for periods of less than a year. Each instance of marginal costing should be documented, setting out how the price has been determined.

It is worth remembering that although marginal cost pricing can sound a good idea, it does not make significant contributions to the running of the Trust. If all prices were at a marginal rate, the Trust would go bankrupt.

Costing and pricing: Concluding comments　Costing and pricing is the most important area to get right. Mistakes in this area can be detrimental to the future viability of your service, your directorate and ultimately your Trust.

BUDGETS AND BUDGETARY INFORMATION

Budget setting　A budget is a method of relating resources, in a Trust's case income received, to expenditure over a period of time – usually a year. Budgets are therefore planned costs which, for the Trust to meet its financial obligations, must equal planned income.

Budgets are normally set on an annual basis. The purpose of this is to identify sources of income and match them to expenditure plans for the following year. In the past this process has started at Christmas but the timetable for the contracting round in the NHS has meant that often budget setting is not completed until well into the financial year to which it relates.

It is possible that this process may be more closely linked to the contracting round when directorates are negotiating their own contracts and therefore their own level of budgets. This seems to be far ahead, but a closer identified relationship between income and budgets is possible and desirable to add incentives into the system for directorates to 'sell' their services successfully and reap some of the rewards.

However, the budget setting timetable should run as shown in Box 3.2.

Box 3.2
The budget setting
timetable

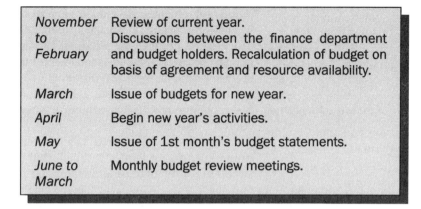

November to February	Review of current year. Discussions between the finance department and budget holders. Recalculation of budget on basis of agreement and resource availability.
March	Issue of budgets for new year.
April	Begin new year's activities.
May	Issue of 1st month's budget statements.
June to March	Monthly budget review meetings.

Staff budgets   To aid negotiations between the budget holder and the finance department, it is important to clarify a few terms.

♦ *Agreed establishment* is the current maximum number of posts within grades against which appointments can be made.
♦ *Funded establishment* is the current number of posts which are funded within a directorate. This would differ from the agreed establishment only if there were unfunded posts.
♦ *Actual establishment* is the current number of staff employed within the directorate. These should not exceed the funded establishment unless there are agreed compensating savings.
♦ *Vacancy factors:* these are often taken away from manpower budgets to reflect the fortuitous savings that can arise from staff turnover, i.e. the delay between one member of staff resigning and a replacement being recruited.

Taking into account all these factors, the manpower budget should equate to the funded establishment less any agreed vacancy factor. It is important to ensure, during negotiations, that funding is agreed for the directorate's manpower.

Non-staff budgets   Most of these budgets are based on the incremental spending levels but may be altered by such items as:

♦ The effects of inflation.
♦ Anticipated developments.
♦ Any non-recurring special items.
♦ Any changes anticipated through increases in activity in the contracting process.
♦ Cost pressures not included in the above.

Remember though, just because a budget was overspent does not automatically mean it can be increased next year. Evidence would have to be presented to the finance department and/or the chief executive to justify an increase. Such evidence could include significant changes in clinical practice; change in case mix or legislative charges. These also need to be input into the pricing process and contract negotiations. Equally if underspent you may need to present a case to avoid losing budget; such evidence could involve problems with recruitment.

The way forward Budgets are much more meaningful when they relate directly to the contract income that is received by the directorate. In this situation, it will follow that any budget deficit must be made up from either taking money from another budget heading (known as virement) or by increasing the contract income for the directorate.

Budgetary information Budgetary information systems are there to aid managers in making rational decisions by identifying past performance and projecting it forwards. This means that the doctor in management has a key role in defining and using this data.

The characteristics of the budgetary information will depend upon the objectives of the users of such information. However, the statements and reports which are produced should contain a combination of the features listed in Box 3.3, the balance being negotiated between managers and accountants.

Box 3.3
Requirements for a
budgetary statement

- ◆ Be accurate.
- ◆ Be timely.
- ◆ Be understandable.
- ◆ Be relevant.
- ◆ Be consistent.
- ◆ Be agreed.
- ◆ Be honest.

Reports need to be accurate to engender confidence in the figures presented and to ensure that decisions are made on the basis of reliable data. Producing reports that are timely increases the usefulness of the information, for instance by allowing time to rectify problems, whereas if such statements are already several weeks out of date it may already be too late for action to be taken.

To be a useful management tool with maximum impact budgetary statements need to be understandable. There should be a relevant level of detail to match the decision-making needs of the user. Reports should, where possible, include narrative to emphasize the messages and graphics to make the information more digestible. This should increase the impact of what is being said.

The reports should be relevant to you. There is little point in generating a report on expenditure you do not control.

Information provided should be consistent, both between time periods to enable meaningful comparisons and between budget holders to ensure 'fair play'.

Report content and format should be agreed by you prior to receipt. This aids the ownership of the information and the decisions which may be prompted upon receipt. The information provided should be seen as honest: for example, a budget statement should include agreed inflation monies.

For effective management decision-making, it is preferable that budgetary information should be combined with other types of data. Integrating budgetary information with manpower data to aid establishment control and, more importantly, with measures of output such as activity information, increases its usefulness and produces a more meaningful basis for decision-making, particularly in the NHS contracting environment. A clinical directorate should be able to relate real income to expenditure, based on finished consultant episodes, via the budgetary control system.

Cost benefit analysis It must be recognized that information costs money and the trade-off between the benefits of improved information, with all of the characteristics discussed above, needs to be compared to the cost of generating and providing that information. There is a need to demonstrate the added value of the information provided in terms of improved decision-making and thereby improved performance of the directorate.

Budgets: Concluding comments Clinical directors can help themselves to obtain the budgetary information they require. Dialogue between the directorate and the management accounts department can help to produce budgetary statements that are user friendly and give the information required. Ask your management accountant for a summary of the directorate position on one side of paper. This will stop the churning out of reams of paper and add a green dimension to your directorate.

CAPITAL CHARGES

Introduction Traditionally in the NHS, capital was seen as a free good. You waited for a number of years for your scheme to come to the top of the list and when it arrived, attempts were made to cure all the ills of the department at the same time. There were no real incentives in the system to use capital wisely or effectively.

In order to create a greater awareness of the cost of capital spending, the concept of capital charges were introduced in 1989. This, for the first time, required hospitals to establish and maintain an asset register and established the cost of capital, comprising two elements:

♦ Depreciation.
♦ Interest.

Depreciation   Depreciation can be defined as the loss of value of the asset incurred through using it for that year. Normally a process known as straight line depreciation is used. A simple example of an x-ray room is illustrated in Box 3.4.

Box 3.4
Straight line
depreciation

Cost of x-ray equipment	£300 000
Life of equipment	12 years
Depreciation = £300 000/12 years = £25 000 per annum	

Interest   The interest part of the capital charge was assessed as being 6%. This was to recognize the fact that capital is no longer a free good and costs money – as anyone with a mortgage will testify.

Therefore, looking at our example of x-ray equipment, the total charge for the year would be as shown in Box 3.5.

Box 3.5
Total capital charges

Depreciation per annum =	£25 000
Interest payment £300 000 × 6%	£18 000
Total capital charge for year	£43 000

Impact   Since 1989, the NHSE has operated a neutral system in applying capital charges in that health authorities have been funded for the capital charges incurred by their Trusts. This is planned to change in 1995/96 and capital charges will become real money.

Both the depreciation and interest elements of capital charges require some form of budgetary control to ensure that the level of actual charges incurred can be monitored against those planned. Although the technology exists to derive capital charges budgets for individual clinical directorates, this rarely occurs, perhaps because capital charges are seen as 'uncontrollable'. However, when making investment decisions at the directorate level, it is reasonable for the director to be held accountable for these decisions and for him or her to see the direct effect on expenditure and prices. Clearly, capital charges do have a direct impact on prices and this should focus thought on the process for making investment decisions (dealt with in the next section).

INVESTMENT
DECISIONS

The day-to-day operation of any clinical directorate requires numerous choices between alternatives. The key is to identify those alternatives and to choose that option which is seen as being best for patient care.

When one looks at investment decisions a similar process of evaluating alternatives needs to take place. Perhaps this is made easier because the immediacy of patient care is not as apparent, but the long-term effects on patient care can be as significant.

This section will focus on investment decisions that involve significant capital spending.

Level of decisions

There are two main levels of decision-making at which choices have to be made. Firstly, the choice between competing needs in the context of constraints on the resources available: for example, whether to invest in a new x-ray room or some cardiac monitoring equipment. Secondly, once the decision is made to go for the x-ray equipment, then a choice needs to be made about what equipment to buy. This may be more than an examination of different suppliers and may involve different solutions.

The first level of choice, deciding between competing needs, is the most difficult. Often no real effort is put into this area and the decision taken is influenced either by table thumping or by position in the queue. An alternative is to make the decision using economic appraisal techniques. This means thinking about the costs and benefits of pursuing or not pursuing each scheme. The costs of the scheme should be easy to identify and include the cost of actually operating the capital. The costs of inaction may be financial, such as increased revenue, but may also include less income or a poorer outcome for patients. The benefits are by definition less easy to quantify and may be more qualitative in nature, such as improved quality or outcome. Exercising choice in this area will prove to be much more challenging. However, the more information that is available the better that decision is likely to be. So find out as much as possible and delve into all the identified effects.

Once this decision is made then the choice of solution can be considered. (Again there is a need to undertake a *cost benefit* appraisal of the options.) This may involve tendering procedures to identify a supplier (see Chapter 2), and it is vitally important that this is done professionally to ensure the right solution is chosen. Again, the financial appraisal is relatively straightforward but the cheapest supplier may well not be the best solution. Care must be taken to consider 'hidden' costs such as maintenance, staffing or energy costs. To ensure the product is the best for the job, a non-financial benefits appraisal needs to be undertaken, preferably with some form of objective scoring against agreed criteria.

This objective scoring becomes important when attempting to distinguish between options when the highest benefit option is not also the lowest cost. An example is worked through in Box 3.6.

Box 3.6
Example of option
appraisal

Total possible points	Non-financial factors	OPTION A	B	C
40	Suitability	30	30	25
40	Durability	10	25	15
20	Compatibility	10	15	20
100	Points score	50	70	60

Financial appraisal		
A	B	C
£400 000	£350 000	£330 000

Clearly Option A is the most expensive and the least beneficial, so it can be discounted. The key decision to make is whether the additional 10 points scored by Option B are worth spending an additional £20 000.

This form of appraisal cannot give a definitive answer in valuing benefit points but it can provide a sensible framework for making the decision.

Investment decisions: Concluding comments

Investment decisions are being made all the time. For significant capital spending it is important that as much information as possible is collected and a formal appraisal is carried out. Only in this way can bad decisions be minimized. Remember, equipment is only replaced every 10 years or so and hospitals perhaps every 100 years, so it is important to take some time to get it right.

TREASURY MANAGEMENT

Importance

Unlike a health authority, which receives an annual allocation of money from the Department of Health, a Trust only receives money to pay its staff and suppliers through contract income. This means that actually receiving the cash from health authorities, GP fund-holders and other customers becomes important to enable the salary bill to be paid and to keep suppliers happy. It also means that items such as stock cost money to retain. For example, if the stocks in a directorate were to be reduced by £50 000 that would generate £50 000 cash to the Trust. With that money the Trust could either pay off some suppliers and potentially receive a greater prompt payment discount or the money could be put in the bank to gain interest, which could be directed at patient care.

Stockholdings It is to everyone's advantage for clinicians to examine stockholdings and potentially rationalize the range of stocks being held in order either to enable a one off cost saving or to obtain greater quantity discounts for those lines left. For the busy clinical director this may seem of little importance but it should be a priority for the directorate's business manager or someone in the finance department.

Strategy The finance department has a responsibility to keep the Trust in a liquid state and able to pay its staff and suppliers. It will need to formulate a strategy based on the following key points:

♦ Secure liquidity at least cost.
♦ Ensure financial stability.
♦ Promote effective and efficient use of resources.
♦ Minimize investment risk.
♦ Only invest cash which is surplus to required working capital.

Long-term At the beginning of this chapter the way in which Trusts are funded
borrowing/ was briefly mentioned. Where the Trust spends more on capital
raising capital than it can fund itself, it may have to borrow to fund its activities. Trusts are not able to use the money market and for long-term borrowing must borrow from the government.
Essentially there are two ways of doing this:

♦ *Public dividend capital (PDC)*. This is a form of long-term government finance on which the government is paid dividends rather than interest. PDC carries no fixed remuneration and is not normally repayable. It is to be remunerated in the long run at a rate at least equal to the rate of interest which would have been set had interest bearing debt been issued instead.
♦ *Interest bearing loans*. A loan cannot be made unless there is a reasonable prospect that it can be serviced and repaid. Lending is at a rate reflecting the government's own credit rating plus a margin for administrative costs. The Secretary of State offers three types of loan:
  – Annual repayment loans
  – Maturity repayment loans
  – Variable rate loans

The rationale behind borrowing only from government is that it is impossible to beat the rate that can be obtained by them on the money markets and therefore it saves the Trust money. It is also a means of keeping tight control of Trust activities.

Treasury Treasury management is clearly an important factor in the manage-
management: ment of a Trust. Although the major decisions will need to be taken
Concluding either by the main board or by the finance department, the
comments activities of the clinical directorate and to a lesser extent the

individual clinician play a major part in maintaining a healthy financial strategy.

VALUE FOR MONEY

Responsibility

Every individual working within the NHS has a responsibility to ensure value for money. The clinical director needs to encourage a culture within the directorate which is based on this responsibility.

The increasing demands made on the NHS have outstripped the willingness and ability of government to pay for these increased demands. Within this context it has been argued that the NHS itself should help to bridge the consequent gap by ensuring that the services provided are delivered as efficiently as possible.

Cost improvement programmes

Most clinicians will have heard of cost improvement programmes (CIPs) in their hospitals. From 1982, as a result of the Griffiths Inquiry, CIPs were built into the funding first of health authorities and, latterly, of Trusts. Since the advent of Trusts, CIPs have tended to be absorbed into the contract negotiation with purchasers. The effect is that a directorate will inevitably be asked to meet a target expressed as either a percentage of budget or a cash sum.

When faced with this issue it is important to be clear just what a CIP is. Box 3.7 lists the main features.

Box 3.7
Cost improvement programmes

♦ Savings must be linked to specific schemes which are accurately costed and recurring in nature (not just the current year).

♦ Achievement of savings should be capable of being monitored.

♦ The schemes should not affect the volume or quality of care. (A ward closure is not a CIP *unless*, for example, it involves a shift to day surgery and total patients treated remains the same or increases.)

♦ Savings generated need to be genuine.

♦ In most instances schemes should be 'cash releasing'. This means achieving the same level of work for less cost. In some cases it is possible to use additional activity but only in the context of meeting higher contract targets.

The internal market mechanism is now the vehicle for promoting CIPs. In essence, this is now through price improvements rather than cost improvements. Unfortunately some commissioners still base contracts on previous costs. It must be better to use the price improvement method: the end point would be the same but it would represent a more logical approach to financial management in the contracting environment. It may also prevent good performers from being penalized, which happens if a straight CIP percentage is demanded from each Trust by a commissioner. Such an approach means that the low cost Trust has to find further savings with potentially less scope to achieve them.

Role of clinicians   It is quite easy to distance yourself from the problem of achieving CIPs. However, it is important to realize that cost savings are a fact of life in the NHS and it is far better to work logically through a directorate's expenditure to identify those areas with potential to save money than to allow a crude management-led approach which may end up being significantly less desirable both for you, the directorate's staff and the patients.

Identification   Once a target level of CIPs has been set, what do you do next? It is likely that there will be some expertise that you can call on within the Trust to assist you in identifying areas for savings. Certainly the finance department should be able to give you assistance, together with your business manager and perhaps your nurse general manager.

A directorate brain-storming session is often a good way to start. It is vital that a positive attitude is taken to assist the process. If some form of reinvestment can take place from a proportion of savings achieved, this is likely to stimulate some enthusiasm. A look at comparative data from similar directorates in other hospitals can also provide useful pointers. You may also, as part of the process, identify potential areas of savings within other directorates with which you work closely. Areas which seem to look promising should then be examined in detail and targets set for the individual budget manager to produce suggestions.

Once all the proposals have been analysed, the effects need to be validated, in terms of both financial effects and effects on patient quality. Where appropriate the effects need to be spelt out. You now have a savings programme.

Value for money: The concepts described above sound very easy on paper. However,
Concluding   a lot of effort, soul-searching and determination will be needed
comments   to achieve the desired result. It may also bring you into conflict with your colleagues and this must be handled sensitively. It must be better to be involved in the process, and ensure that it is carried out rationally, than to leave it to others outside the directorate who may cause considerable disruption and arrive at a less optimal solution.

MAKING THE BEST USE OF YOUR FINANCE DEPARTMENT

You are not alone

Quite often, particularly when faced with a seemingly intractable problem, it is difficult to feel anything other than that it is your problem. In the case of a clinical dilemma, this may be so but in matters of financial management this should not be so. The role of a finance department is not to be stuck inside an ivory tower, finding yet more frustrating ways of saying 'no' to everything that comes across their desks. The modern finance department should be there to help you, acting as a facilitator, if not always as a paymaster. The answer you get should be 'yes, you need to consider this', rather than 'no'.

Availing yourself of the finance department is, however, a two-way process. Ask yourself some questions:

♦ Do you know who your finance director is?
♦ Do you know who looks after your directorate in the finance department?
♦ Do you know where to find them?

If you answer 'no' to all or some of these questions, then you know what to do. It may be appropriate to invite a representative to your directorate meetings. Involve yourself in building up the relationship. Do not just assume your business manager or nurse general manager will do it for you. If you have a decent finance person, he or she will be delighted to become more involved in the workings of your part of the service. Finance people often feel out of the hustle and bustle of a busy directorate and welcome opportunities to get involved in topical issues.

Once contact has been made and a relationship established, you will find that it pays dividends on a number of fronts. Those annoying things that keep appearing on your statements without explanation will suddenly disappear and you will feel more confidence in the figures that are presented to you. You will also find someone to help you when the chief executive wants to know some answers, or asks a number of 'what if' questions.

Other help

Finance departments also provide a number of documents which may be helpful in finding your way through the systems and processes of the Trust. The main source is the 'Standing Financial Instructions' (SFIs). These should be available within the directorate and are an important reference document. Although they are often thick documents, a look at the contents page should assist in directing you to areas such as contracting, purchasing, budgets and budgetary control principles. Often finance departments also produce budget holder guidance which expands on the principles identified in SFIs and takes you through the processes of agreeing a budget and how to get it altered.

Finance department: Concluding comments Finance staff are there to help and not to hinder you in achieving your objectives. They are a valuable resource who, in the main, will be interested in your problems and willing to help solve them.

CONCLUSION This chapter has attempted to highlight a number of issues which will be of relevance to the clinician in management. Given the limited space it is not possible to do complete justice to each of them. However, it is hoped that you will use this as a springboard to tackle this difficult area.

The key message is that you are not alone – there are plenty of people in your directorate or finance department who have the skills to help you perform your financial duties. It will pay considerable dividends to build a relationship with them and have them by your side and at your meetings.

Aspects of finance, in common with areas in any profession, can be very complex. However, being aware of the basic constraints of the system will help you to understand the way in which the NHS works and should avoid you going up too many blind alleys. It is important to have a knowledge of the systems in place so that you can ensure that your directorate is not disadvantaged by not realizing what it should be demanding of its finance department.

SUMMARY

To summarize the points made in this chapter:

♦ Finance is key to understanding some of the concepts of management.
♦ Expenditure *must* equal income from contracts.
♦ There are three key financial targets for a Trust
  - Break-even.
  - Make a 6% return on assets.
  - Meet the Trust's external financing limit.
♦ The NHSE keeps a firm grip on the finances of Trusts.
♦ Prices should be based on costs.
♦ Prices must be right to ensure future viability.
♦ It is important to understand the budget setting process.
♦ You should demand budgetary information that is accurate, timely and understandable.
♦ Capital costs money, it is not a 'free' good.
♦ Only make investment decisions when you have adequate information and ideally only after a formal appraisal has been carried out.
♦ The ability of a Trust to pay its staff and suppliers is dependent on contract income coming in.
♦ Stocks should be rationalized and minimized.

- ◆ Value for money must be on the agenda of everyone in the directorate.
- ◆ It is important that you are involved in the CIP process.
- ◆ Finance staff are there to help not hinder you. They are a valuable resource, use them.

FURTHER READING

- ◆ Bromwich, M. (1976), *The Economics of Capital Budgeting*, Penguin, London.

A readable explanation of how to evaluate options.

- ◆ Drummond, M.F. (1985), *Principles of Economic Appraisal in Health Care*, Oxford University Press, Oxford.

Takes Bromwich's financial basis and looks at option appraisal more fully from an economic benefit point of view.

- ◆ Mellett, H., Marriott, N. and Harries, S. (1993), *Financial Management in the NHS*, Chapman & Hall, London.

One of the few books to encompass the whole range of NHS financial management and provides good information on budgets and budget setting.

- ◆ Perrin, J. (1988), *Resource Management in the NHS*, Van Nostrand Reinhold (UK), London.

Looks more closely at the links between budgets and activity and, although now somewhat dated, is still of use in establishing budgets.

MANAGING PEOPLE

Peter Barnes

OBJECTIVES

- ◆ To develop an understanding of how people function inside large organizations.
- ◆ To use this understanding to show how the clinical manager can act as motivator, team builder, and supporter of staff development.
- ◆ To demonstrate that there is no easy prescription for managing people and no substitute for vision, trust and communication.

INTRODUCTION

This chapter deals with some aspects of a subject that involves each of us every day but at which few of us are skilled: managing people. People constitute the major resource of the health service. Many of them will be our working colleagues for a very long time and yet we often treat this asset with less regard than we would cheap and replaceable equipment. We would not willingly use a piece of kit for the wrong job, for no good reason, for far too long, with no maintenance and without update and if we did and it let us down we would probably blame ourselves. But with people we behave differently. It is no wonder that we occasionally hear of 'a colleague from hell'.

It could be you.

Setting the scene

The Unit Management Board meeting eventually finished at 8 p.m. After a series of often difficult and thought provoking meetings the new organizational structure had finally been agreed. The Board itself had been slimmed down in size and in general the management structure was flatter and now involved more doctors in an expanded clinical directorate system. All that was necessary now was to give the changes wide publicity within the hospital. It was the most fundamental reorganization since the introduction of general management a number of years previously.

The next week in the staff restaurant a newly appointed radiographer was asking her senior colleagues what sort of place the hospital was. 'It's very busy' she was told 'and we're going to be a Trust in the next wave. The managers have been working on a number of changes and they keep sending out loads of information. Our boss is going to be called clinical director but I don't think that will affect us really. You will find it's quite a friendly place, very different from the last place I worked in'.

The second radiographer had highlighted an essential difference between the two hospitals where she had worked, in this case friendliness, that no organizational chart could show. Every organization has a culture of its own, a corporate 'personality'. In large organizations several different cultures can exist at the same time. Furthermore 'there are deep set beliefs about the way work should be organized, the way authority should be exercised, people rewarded, people controlled. What are the degrees of formalization required? How much planning and how far ahead? What combination of obedience and initiative is looked for in subordinates? Do work hours matter, or dress, or personal eccentricities? Do committees control or individuals? Are there rules and procedures or only results?' (Handy, 1985).

The complex relationships that exist in large organizations have been described in terms of both the internal and external environment (Nadler and Tushman, 1980). Internally the organization is seen to be composed of four elements:

◆ The tasks: the jobs and activities which need to be carried out if the organization is to achieve its goals.
◆ The formal structure: lines of accountability, job definitions, organization, operating policies etc. The job as it looks on paper.
◆ The informal structure: less tangible and more enduring than the formal arrangements. Who has what influence and why. Who is in and who is out. The real organization alive and functioning.
◆ The individuals: the people who bring knowledge skills, values and behaviour and all the personal differences that influence the achievements of the organization.

Externally the organization is seen to react with the environment by initiating change and responding to pressures. Recent examples of significant external pressures affecting hospitals include the development of the internal market, the Patient's Charter, demands for changing clinical practice and the problems of junior doctors' hours. These changes have had considerable consequences for the four internal elements of the organization.

The Nadler and Tushman model also hints at the need for leadership to coordinate all the activities of the organization and to produce a shared vision of a better future without which successful change cannot occur.

Managers have often been described as people who get their work done through others. In the context of consultant firms the work is usually self-evident and the team members self-motivating. Consultants over the period of their training have inevitably acquired some skills in communication, performance-monitoring and service organization but usually within fairly narrow clinical boundaries. Changing clinical practice, improving technology and increasing demands from purchasers and patients are all creating the need to understand the wider clinical team, the relationships with other clinical teams in the organization and the vital contribution of non-clinical services to effective patient care. When the difficulty of resource constraint is added to the list and quality and waiting list targets are mandatory the management challenge can seem overwhelming.

Casually acquired management skills are unlikely to be adequate.

Effective clinical managers need the ability to build and motivate a team, set clear and realistic targets for success and monitor progress. To do this they must be able to relate to people as individuals and as groups and manage themselves and their own time as effectively as their team. *They must become experts not only at managing patients but also managing people.*

MANAGING CLINICAL TEAMS

Clinical management involves the identification of a range of financial and other resources available to provide patient care and the assurance that these resources are utilized to greatest effect for the benefit of the individual patient and groups of patients (Harwood and Boufford, 1993). At the heart of the concept of clinical management, as it is now practised in the UK, is the clinical management team.

Typically the management team includes a clinical director, (usually, but not necessarily a consultant), a business manager and a professional manager, for example, a nurse or technical manager. Descriptions of accountability vary and in the case of the doctors it is often quite vague. Many clinical directors do not really feel accountable to the chief executive in spite of the structure set out on paper and few consultants at present regard themselves as accountable to the clinical director. However, the clinical director may be required by the Board to achieve certain results. How can this be accomplished?

Power is the ability to impose one's will or to control or influence others. Authority is the right to use this power. Legitimate authority, power delegated by the chief executive to clinical directors, may be necessary but in most cases better results will be obtained by generating agreement about the task and motivating and supporting the team and its members in its execution.

A good manager will understand the interplay between the task, the team and the individual.

Task   Task is an unfamiliar word in the health service. Aim and objective are better understood. Objective describes discrete, tangible and measurable outcomes limited in time. Objectives are SMART:

- ◆ *S*pecific
- ◆ *M*easurable
- ◆ *A*chievable
- ◆ *R*ealistic
- ◆ *T*imed

An aim is less defined but likely to be substantial and usually describes a longer-term goal.

To accomplish a task the manager must not only understand the brief but communicate it to the group. The team must know what needs to be done and why. The manager and the team together agree an action plan and a monitoring system is devised. In addition the manager must recognize 'downward accountability' and ensure that the necessary resources are available to enable the team to perform well.

Team   In order to perform well the team will need to sense a realistic possibility of achievement and develop high morale. Success breeds success and to sustain high performance a team will need to be presented with still more challenging tasks. In order to get the team to this level of performance the manager must:

- ◆ Monitor progress giving constructive feedback and praising achievement.
- ◆ Understand the informal culture.
- ◆ Resolve conflict positively.
- ◆ Demonstrate appropriate loyalty.
- ◆ Develop mutual trust and a sense of common purpose.

It is easier to build team spirit when you are winning but more necessary when you are losing.

Individuals   Individual employees bring with them their own needs not just for financial reward but for self-fulfilment and social relationships. They will probably know where they stand in the formal organizational arrangements and where they fit into the informal culture. Some will have specific beliefs that may hinder satisfactory completion of a given task. A good manager will pay particular attention to the individuals in the team and will:

- ◆ Specify what the task requires.
- ◆ Ensure ability, knowledge and skills are appropriate.

◆ Recognize individual achievement.
◆ Help the individual to avoid being overwhelmed by the task or the team.

MOTIVATION Members joining your team on their first day will not expect to be paid the most for doing the least, get away with doing the bare minimum or go home feeling unhappy, unfulfilled and frustrated. Most people feel enthusiastic, hope for success and are motivated to work.

A cynical view is that people are motivated by fear, power or excitement or a combination of these. However, more sophisticated theories exist. One suggests a hierarchy of needs ranging from basic physiological and safety needs to higher order needs, for example, self-actualization. We would recognize this hierarchy as:

◆ Physical security.
◆ Social belonging.
◆ Status.
◆ Achievement.
◆ Recognition.

This theory proposes that needs become motivators when they are unsatisfied and lower order needs dominate until they are met. Experience suggests that whilst this is true at the basic level, needs at a number of different levels can operate at the same time. The need to be accepted as a member of a group, to have particular talents or skills recognized and to have a sense of self-fulfilment can all coexist.

McGregor (1966) offered alternative assumptions about human behaviour which may underlie much managerial action. These assumptions are described as theory-X and theory-Y.

In summary theory-X suggests that:

◆ On average, humans have an inherent dislike of work. Therefore management needs to stress productivity and incentive schemes.
◆ People will need to be coerced, directed and threatened with punishment.
◆ The average human prefers to be directed, wishes to avoid responsibility, has little ambition and wants security above all.

Theory-Y suggests:

◆ The ordinary person does not dislike work, which can be as natural as play or rest and a source of satisfaction.
◆ People exercise self-control and self-direction in the pursuit of objectives.
◆ Under appropriate circumstances most will not only accept but seek responsibility. Many more people are able to contribute

creatively to the solution of organizational problems than at present do so.

♦ At present the potentialities of the average person are not being fully used.

♦ The most significant reward that can be offered in order to obtain commitment is the satisfaction of the individual's self-actualizing needs.

These latter points are of extreme importance. They suggest that people can be stretched in efforts directed towards organizational objectives in a way that is of personal significance to them. They will regard their jobs and their contribution to the objectives as meaningful, indispensable and challenging. In order to do this work they will need the support of their superiors, and managers will need to take on this supporting role.

A third approach was suggested by Herzberg who described two different sets of features which can influence the way people feel about their jobs (Hertzberg, 1966). One set of factors can produce dissatisfaction but provide little motivation. The second set of factors are those which may produce motivation.

Things which may produce dissatisfaction include status, working conditions and features of company policy and administration. When these are inappropriate hardly a day will go by without some complaint about administrative policy, bureaucracy, the physical environment, inadequate equipment or car parking arrangements. Correcting the faults will reduce dissatisfaction but only have a neutral effect on motivation.

Motivators, already alluded to, include achievement, recognition, responsibility and advancement.

The role of salary is less clear. An increase in salary is often given in response to expressed dissatisfaction and may be given as a reward for apparent success as in the merit award system. Senior health service managers are now giving serious consideration to the introduction of performance related pay.

There are well recognized problems with both of these systems which probably relate not to the absolute level of pay but to the perceived unfairness of the system in which one worker is rewarded and another not for apparently equal work.

In both systems there is the possibility that the success which has been rewarded has been built on the efforts of others. For performance related pay it may be much more sensible to introduce a system in which the role of all the individuals in the team is recognized and all the group is rewarded when it achieves its targets. Celebrating the success of the team in this way can be a potent team building exercise.

At clinical directorate level the ability to use financial inducement is limited but many of the other features concerned with motivation and demotivation are within the control of the clinical director. The reality is that motivation arises not only within the individual but also from the team and the task itself. Managing the overlap between the task, the team and the individual is a challenging and rewarding opportunity. A good manager will:

♦ achieve the task
♦ build the team
♦ develop the individual

BUILDING THE TEAM

A team is a group of people working together for common purpose. Prerequisites for success are:

♦ Clear aims.
♦ Careful planning.
♦ The ability to work together.

In a detailed study of management teams Belbin identified a number of key roles which together would advance the team process effectively (Belbin, 1981) (Box 4.1).

You will probably recognize some of these characteristics in yourself and your colleagues.

Most people are capable of having more than one of these characteristics but all have a dominant style. In small teams members may contribute to more than one of these roles. It is likely that teams, big or small, will find they have problems when there are gaps in the team, when one person is taking on too many roles or when a person is taking the wrong role. It may be necessary to add to the team additional members with known characteristics to help complete the task.

Very often the teams are a 'given' with membership determined by status or special experience. The team leader will then face the problem of trying to get the task accomplished at the same time as getting the individuals to work together as a team. Groups put together in such a way usually undergo a series of fairly well recognized changes before working at their best. It is useful for the team leader to recognize these changes before interfering with the membership of the team. Stages can be described as in Box 4.2.

These stages mirror a life cycle from infancy through adolescence to maturity and occasionally euthanasia.

LEADING THE TEAM

The success of your team will be significantly influenced by your attributes and style as team leader. The way you relate to the group is of crucial importance but these relationships may need to vary from time to time. The determinants of success are not always easy to identify. One group working with a strong authoritarian leader may achieve significant results. Another, with similar management style, may break up in disarray. Shared informal leadership can be associated with either excellent team play or indecisiveness and

Box 4.1
Useful people to have
in teams

Type	Typical features	Positive qualities	Allowable weakness
Implementor	Conservative, dutiful, predictable	Organizing ability, practical common sense, hard-working, self-discipline	Lack of flexibility, unresponsiveness to unproven ideas
Coordinator	Calm, self-confident, controlled	A capacity for treating and welcoming all potential contributors on their merits and without prejudice. A strong sense of objectives	No more than ordinary in terms of intellect or creative ability
Shaper	Highly strung, outgoing	Drive and readiness to challenge inertia, ineffectiveness, complacency or self-deception	Proneness to provocation, irritation and impatience
Plant	Individualistic, serious-minded, unorthodox	Genius, imagination, intellect, knowledge	Up in the clouds, inclined to disregard practical details or protocol
Resource investigator	Extroverted, enthusiastic, curious	A capacity for contacting people and exploring anything new. An ability to respond to challenge	Liable to lose interest once the initial fascination has passed
Monitor evaluator	Sober, unemotional, prudent	Judgement, discretion, hard-headedness	Lacks inspiration or the ability to motivate others
Team worker	Socially orientated, rather mild	An ability to respond to people and to situations, and to promote harmony	Indecisiveness at moments of crisis
Specialist	Single-minded, self-starting	Brings knowledge or skills in rare supply	Contributes only on narrow front
Completer/ finisher	Painstaking, orderly, conscientious, anxious	A capacity for follow through. Perfectionism	A tendency to worry about small things. A reluctance to 'let go'

Box 4.2
Stages in group
development

♦ *Forming*: members find out who they are and what they can do. Establish basic criteria and behaviour. Dependent on leader. Low contribution.

♦ *Storming*: conflicts develop, subgroups form, resistance to task, insubordination. Noisy.

♦ *Warming*: warming to task, exchange of ideas, cohesion. Listening.

♦ *Performing*: settled interdependence, seeking agreement, problem-solving. Bonding.

♦ *Transforming*: new goals, redefinition of group or task completed. Termination.

confusion. What is certain is that without effective leadership the group is likely to have no sense of direction, purpose or motivation.

Managers are people too. You will have your own needs, personality and problems. You will also have your own preferred management style. Good managers however will vary the style according to the demands of the task and the needs of the group or individual they are working with.

Management styles with which clinicians are familiar involve direction, education and delegation.

Direction Authoritarian management, telling others what to do, is vital when urgent decisions need to be made. It is the style most easily recognized as leadership and attractive to those who need to demonstrate their position or power. It works when used appropriately. Overuse produces real problems. The team loses the ability or the inclination to prioritize work appropriately and become dependent upon the whim of the manager. The manager, always telling people what to do, has no time or inclination to listen to the team members. Eventually the ability to listen is lost. The team stops developing and motivation dwindles. In the absence of the boss, performance is poor.

Education Educational management, encouraging the team to come up with the right answer, is crucial to team development. The decision is clearly based on what the manager wants but the team or the individual feel a sense of ownership. The manager may have had to lead the discussion in a particular direction, emphasize relevant facts, even sell the idea to the team. In the process the team have all signed up to the required action and have learned from the experience. Confidence has been built and the ground has been prepared for further development. In future the manager will not have to spend as much time in supervising similar tasks.

Delegation Education has paved the way for delegation. The manager is in a position to hand out work to others who are known to be capable of doing it. Delegation is not abdication. It has to be done responsibly and with the confidence that the person can handle the work on their own initiative with help and advice available if required.

It is wrong to delegate work unless you are willing to give the necessary authority and resources, including time, to accomplish the task and be explicit as to how progress will be monitored.

Effective delegation has several advantages: it enhances morale, motivation, learning and, equally importantly, frees up a manager's time. Continual managerial interference in the task prevents these outcomes.

Democratic leadership This is a style of leadership that many clinicians have difficulty in accepting. The leader under these circumstances functions as an equal member of the group, each member bringing to it their expert knowledge. The leader may act as coordinator of the group but sometimes another team member or even an outsider may be called upon to serve as a facilitator. This style has particular importance in activities involving problem-solving techniques such as brainstorming.

Unfortunately in problem-solving meetings clinicians are often seen to dominate when present and typically identify the solution before the problem has been fully worked out. This is not something that they would normally do when faced with problems in clinical practice. A dominant stance by the leader will inhibit the contribution of others, lead to failure of the diagnostic process and inevitably to the wrong prescription.

Leading by example Whatever leadership style is used the leader will always be looked upon to a greater or lesser extent as a model for the team. The team is unlikely to sustain higher standards than those of the leader – if it does the leader will not long be in office.

In a study of doctors who excelled in management, the competencies that separated excellent from merely good performers were examined (Turrel, 1993). The features listed in Box 4.3 were identified with sufficient frequency to suggest that they are important qualities.

Box 4.3
Features of successful leaders

♦ Achieving – demonstrating enterprise and initiative.

♦ Thinking – thinking analytically.

♦ Influencing – influencing strategically, persuading rationally.

These factors describe particular abilities. In a good leader they will be used in pursuit of the team's goals. The team will respond better if they know that this is so; that they can trust the leader who is acting on their behalf and that this trust is reciprocated.

In order to generate an atmosphere of trust the team leader will need to perform with:

◆ Openness.
◆ Consistency.
◆ Reliability.

MAKING THE BEST OF THE TEAM   The team is assembled, a well chosen group of people of appropriate ability working towards a common goal. What can go wrong?

Some members will have a degree of influence out of proportion to their ability in the particular task. Professional hierarchies and the informal culture will need to be well understood.

Frequent contributors often have high influence but some people talk a lot and are not listened to. Others may say little but when they speak have the attention of all. Some members may actively exude pessimism and have a significant negative influence. Enthusiasts can lead the discussion beyond realistic boundaries. Individuals or sub-groups may 'know the answer' and try to force it through against the wishes of others or without appropriate exploration.

The know-all, the show-off and the bully will all make an appearance from time to time.

It is the manager's role to gain the support and commitment of those of high influence and minimize the impact of the pessimists. Conflicts and rivalry should be identified early and be diffused or dealt with positively. Sometimes other members of the group will help to maintain group morale, drawing members into discussion and refocusing on the task.

Of particular danger for small groups is the emergence of 'group think'. Too high a value is placed on harmony and thinking becomes blinkered. Such groups are quick to rationalize factors which do not fit with their policies, to stereotype enemies and to exhibit inappropriate loyalty. Collective responsibility is invoked to stifle dissent outside the group. Poor communication with other teams in the hospital can be both a symptom and a cause of group think.

The risks can be reduced by the deliberate introduction of outsiders into the group. Most Trust Boards will have felt the impact of non-executive members on their thinking style and many clinical directors who have been in close contact with, for example, GP fundholders will have had their ideas challenged and probably modified.

The environment   A team can only work together if it gets together. Physical proximity increases interaction and this usually promotes cooperation. For routine work, team members should either have offices close together or find a suitable venue where they can meet on a regular basis. It is unrealistic to expect good results with inadequate resources. For a short time people can rise above the circumstances. Discomfort can produce high cohesion, hence the popularity of 'outward bound' management training schemes. In the long term, however, poor circumstances are demotivating and people treated in a second rate manner will deliver a second rate service.

The right mental environment is as important as the physical environment and time spent away from the workplace is important. Meeting off site away from the psychological pressures of work, bleep-free and mobile phone-free, can have a significant effect on team building and team productivity. Time to think clearly about new problems, generate new ideas and plan effectively is time well spent. Busy clinicians often find it difficult to justify taking time out. The consequence can often be that ultimately more time is spent in fire fighting than would have been spent if the problem had been dealt with properly at the outset.

TEAM THINKING   One of the features of groups is that they produce fewer ideas in total than the individuals in those groups working separately. In general, however, the ideas are better in the sense that they are better evaluated and more refined.

A quiz team will produce a better result than an individual because, collectively, it knows more than the best single performer. When it comes to problem-solving, however, there is the imperative of recognizing the real nature of the problem; asking the right question. It is common for managers to hear the question phrased in terms of the preconceived notion of the solution. 'The problem is we have not got enough beds' ergo, the answer is to give more beds. Further analysis may well reveal that the real problem is difficulty in discharging patients because of inadequate resources in the community. Involving members of the team in identifying the real question is more likely to lead to correct identification of the problem and therefore to the best solution.

Since there may be more than one good solution, a number of ideas will be generated and their value will have to be assessed in terms of effective outcomes. Only one idea will be selected after this evaluation and therefore most ideas will have to be rejected. The manager must learn to handle this in such a way that the authors of the discarded ideas do not themselves feel rejected and will continue to contribute their ideas to the team in the future.

Managers operate in an uncertain world and one of the functions of management is to reduce uncertainty to a level at which a

Box 4.4
The decision-making process

> *Stage 1 – the question.*
> Formulate (or reformulate) the question, to address the issues in the clearest possible way. Gather relevant information.
>
> *Stage 2 – the alternatives.*
> Create the most effective range of alternatives to answer the question.
>
> *Stage 3 – the consequences.*
> Predict the future consequences of acting on each of the alternative answers, consider contingency plans in case the choice proves to be wholly or partially wrong.
>
> *Stage 4 – the decision.*
> Traditional decision-making. Balancing the risk and reward offered by each alternative and using judgement to decide.

sensible decision can be taken. The decision-making process has been clearly described by Heirs (1989) (Box 4.4).

Once the decision has been taken in this way the action should be implemented.

It is easy to think without acting and not uncommon to act without thinking. At times we have all been guilty of both of these mistakes.

The manager must ensure that thought precedes action and that people who work together as a team must first learn how to think together as a team.

CONFLICT HANDLING

Even in the best managed teams conflict arises from time to time. Managers are more likely to avoid conflicts developing within the team when they:

♦ Avoid creating win/lose situations between team members.
♦ Make it clear what is expected of team members.
♦ Involve the team as much as possible in decision-making.
♦ Have developed a sense of trust within the team.

When conflict does arise in your team you will be tempted to follow one of three courses. You could ignore the problem. If it was a minor grievance this may turn out to be the best course of action but you may have run the risk of ignoring what was the tip of an iceberg.

You could 'buy off' one of the protagonists. The problem appears to have been solved but the underlying cause will remain and you are now in debt to one of your colleagues.

You could work out 'the solution' and impose it. In doing so you have abused your legitimate authority, failed to solve the real problem and created at least one more: resentment of your solution.

If the problem is more one of perception than reality simply getting the people involved to work together on a different problem may be all that is necessary. This will provide an opportunity for peace signals to be passed and allow them to get to know each other better and to understand each other's point of view. This may not always lead to a complete and satisfactory resolution of the problem and in some cases may aggravate interpersonal relationships.

Sooner or later you will have to face the problem of dealing with a difficult colleague. To tackle the problem it must be seen rationally. In most situations the difficulty arises because the colleague (A) is not performing in the way that the organization requires. A number of questions stem from this (Box 4.5).

Box 4.5
Dealing with a difficult colleague

♦ Does A have clear agreed objectives? (That is, know what the organization requires.)

♦ Is A able to achieve these objectives?
(If not, does A require:

> information
> facilities
> staff
> time
> training
> help)

NB: If you are A's manager all of these are within your remit and should have been dealt with initially, in other words, A's problem is of your making.

♦ Is A prevented from performing? (by whom or by what)

♦ Is A ill or in trouble?

♦ Is disciplinary action necessary?

It will probably now be clear what needs to be done and whose responsibility it is.

If the problem is yours to tackle, do not delegate the role to someone else. You will diminish your standing and authority, be less able to resolve future problems and probably fail to resolve this one. You will need to meet A to discuss the matter. As the manager you hold the advantage. You have prepared the ground and should now be quite clear about your own intentions. You can offer A a number of times and places for interview ensuring that these are convenient to you whilst at the same time appearing to be reasonable. Allow enough time for the interview and make sure neither of you is going to be interrupted. Explain the purpose of the interview beforehand so that A cannot use lack of preparation as an excuse to procrastinate. Listen carefully to A's side of the argument then firmly state your position based on reason rather than emotion. At the end of the meeting agree what has been resolved and what, if anything, remains to be dealt with. Agree a timetable for outstanding issues. Do not allow yourself to be filibustered into non-resolution of the problem. The overwhelming majority of problems can be sorted out by rational discussion. Particular problems can arise with peers whose view of service needs is different from those of the organization. It should be possible to prevent this sort of problem arising in the future by proper and adequate consultation in the business planning process.

It is rarely necessary to resort to disciplinary procedures. Medical managers are often out of their depth in these matters. As with any other difficult diagnostic or therapeutic problem you should take specialist advice and consult the personnel department. This, after all, is one of the things they are paid to deal with.

STAFF SELECTION

Many doctors have had experience of staff selection interviews on both sides of the table. We regard ourselves as being skilled at interviewing; we do it all the time with our patients. And yet, even now, a candidate can write 'the experience was more of a farce than an assessment' (Edgell, 1994). The general experience of doctors in staff selection has centred round discussions over short-listing and taking part in the actual selection interview. A medical manager's role should start much earlier with discussion about whether a vacancy needs to be filled at all.

There are three basic questions:

◆ Do we need another person?
◆ What do we want them to do?
◆ Who do we need to do it?

Do we need another person?

There seems to be an automatic assumption that when a member of staff leaves a replacement is required. Changing demands, advances in technology, differing working practices, spare capacity elsewhere may all make reappointment unnecessary. Conversely, increasing pressures to perform, waiting list problems and additional equipment may all create the need for new jobs. A sound business case for every appointment should now be regarded as a sine qua non.

Job description Having decided that a vacancy really exists, a job analysis should be undertaken. This would ideally include a post holder of a similar job, some others with whom the employee would work and the appropriate supervisor or manager. Advice from the personnel department is essential. The analysis should lead to the complete description of the purpose, duties and relationships of the job, specifying the tasks and the skills necessary, the physical and mental demands of the work, the working environment and the terms and conditions of service.

Person specification The health service is labour intensive. It depends heavily on people to do the work and getting the wrong person in post could be an expensive mistake. Drawing up a profile of the ideal candidate can be a helpful aid to selection. Many of the requirements flow naturally from a well prepared job description. Minimum criteria can be laid down in terms of essential and desirable characteristics. These will cover areas such as education, attainment, previous experience and ability and personal circumstances relevant to the post; for example, ability to work unsociable hours or in a smoke-free environment.

In order to select the best field of candidates the job description and person specification should not include criteria irrelevant to good performance and must not discriminate on the basis of race or sex. Advertising should be appropriate for the job and the expected field of candidates. Short-listing procedures should be based on the person specifications and candidates successful at this stage should be called for interview.

Interview The interview is a competitive process. Only one person will be appointed for each post and candidates understand this and will accept the outcome if the process is seen to be fair. Complaints about bias or unfairness in selection are increasing and inter-viewers individually and collectively must be able to justify their decision. Note keeping is essential.

The interview itself should be carefully planned with an appropriate venue and adequate notice and information for the candidates. Sufficient time must be allowed. If it is a panel interview members should meet in good time beforehand and agree what they are looking for. Candidates are being assessed for their:

- Eligibility.
- Capability.
- Suitability.

Eligibility should have been covered by the short-listing process. The interview process should therefore further explore capability and suitability.

Conducting the interview   The candidates should be put at ease (as far as possible) and the interview process explained. The order of questions should have been agreed beforehand. The members of the interviewing team will have been introduced at the beginning but should be introduced again individually as the interview proceeds. Each interviewer should ask the prepared questions and supplementary questions as necessary, taking notes as unobtrusively as possible. The interviewer should listen to the answers (why else ask all the questions), and note the candidate's body language. All interviewers should remember that the candidate will be noting their body language too whether or not they are the ones asking questions. Non-verbal behaviour too commonly encountered at selection interviews includes interviewers looking at their watch, continually shuffling papers and staring out the window.

More will be learned of the candidate by asking questions which are open rather than closed. Many questions relate to past performance but if potential is being assessed, situational or problem centred questions can be helpful.

It is important that panel members should only ask questions when invited to do so by the chair of the panel. Until this happens panel members should pay attention to the question being asked by their colleague and the answers being given but should remain quiet. When a member has finished asking questions they should indicate this to the chair. The chair may then ask other panel members whether they have questions they wish to ask the candidate on the specific topic being discussed, particularly if the selection panel is small. The questioning is then passed on to the next interviewer.

When the interview is finally brought to a close the candidate should be given the opportunity to ask questions and then informed of any necessary further steps and when a decision is likely to be reached.

The decision   Ideally each member should write up his or her notes and rate the candidates independently.

Judgements will need to be made about current ability and the potential for development. Poor attainment in one area may be more than compensated for by abilities elsewhere. Personality issues with regard to team building may favour one candidate over another. Will the candidate rock the boat or can they fit into the team without disturbing its good function? Conversely it may be thought that the team is too cosy, too harmonious and that the boat needs to be rocked. If so has the candidate the strength of personality to avoid being submerged in group think?

The panel should review and discuss their individual assessment and scores and evaluate the evidence. Finally, they should make a joint panel decision. Decisions should be formally recorded, including reasons for:

◆ Choosing the successful candidate.
◆ Rejecting unsuccessful candidates.
◆ Appointing a second candidate if the preferred candidate fails to take up the appointment.

All records including notes made by the selectors should be retained for at least six months.

Feedback to unsuccessful candidates is an essential part of the interview process and an appropriate member of the interview panel should be responsible for providing this feedback.

Does the interview achieve its purpose? There is much evidence that decisions are made by individual interviewers in the first two or three minutes of the interview. The rest of the time seems to be spent in seeking confirmatory evidence for this rapidly reached opinion. The use of larger panels can even out this bias but usually at the risk of producing a less 'satisfying' interview. However, the two areas where interviews produce the most valid judgements are in relation to motivation and personal relationships, features which contribute significantly to the person's suitability for the post.

But perhaps the interview is best seen as one, albeit important, step in the career development of the successful candidate. The interview, indeed the whole selection process, can be regarded as a means of identifying relevant training needs for the new employee. On both sides there is then the recognition that training and development is expected. Meeting this need will enhance job satisfaction and motivation and help bind the new employee to the organization.

STAFF DEVELOPMENT

As we have already seen, achievement, responsibility and advancement are significant motivators for most people. Furthermore, improving the ability of staff will improve effectiveness and efficiency without necessarily increasing costs. Training of non-medical staff as in the case of medical staff depends not only on continuing experience but tuition, access to appropriate courses and time for personal study. Ample opportunity for continuing education is provided for medical staff whose training goals are usually easy to identify. Matters are less straightforward for other staff but the need is as great to develop people's ability to do the job now and in the future. A number of professions in the NHS are strictly regulated with regard to professional qualifications. These include doctors and dentists, nurses, professions allied to medicine and pharmacists amongst others. In addition a wide range of staff, for example medical physics technicians, physiological measurement technicians and medical laboratory assistants, receive formal vocational training. Qualification within the national vocational qualification (NVQ) scheme is being extended to include some groups which at present have no formal training. It cannot be expected that the typical clinical or medical director will have intimate knowledge of all of these schemes or of their application. It is important, however, to recognize that training needs exist and to explore with the human resource department how they can be met.

Staff development almost by definition should be a continuous process. There are, however, specific circumstances when relevant training becomes of paramount importance.

♦ Induction training for new employees. In general these have been better recognized and managed in non-medical rather than medical sectors. Induction schemes for new house officers are now mandatory.
♦ Training in the use of new equipment or new systems.
♦ Training in relation to promotion, for example, in managerial skills.

These three areas highlight the role of education, training and development in enabling individuals to fulfil their organizational responsibilities. Difficulties arise when the demands on time of the individual cause friction within the team. In order to avoid this the training and development of staff should be linked to the business planning process. Managers should reconcile the needs of individuals with those of the organization as far as possible and establish realistic expectations of what can be achieved.

The clinical manager will usually find that the business manager and nurse or professional manager fully understand the training provision for their specialist groups. Much help will be gained from the human resources department. Nevertheless it is the ultimate responsibility of the clinical manager to ensure for the staff in the team:

♦ The identification and prioritization of training needs.
♦ Training provision and its funding.
♦ Evaluation of the training.

Clinical managers will need a working knowledge of current agreements on reducing doctors' hours, continuing medical education for consultants, 'working paper 10' arrangements for the education of non-medical professions and the NVQ schemes.

MULTI-SKILLING   An obvious time when training should be specific and targeted is when staff are being encouraged to take on new roles. It is fashionable at present to talk about multi-skilling, but in practice this commonly means asking one group of workers to perform tasks previously done by others. Acceptance varies. For example, in some departments nurses willingly take blood samples or perform electrocardiograms and in others will not do so. Yet many basic tasks can easily be performed by anybody with appropriate training: the advantage in terms of efficiency of generic workers capable of undertaking a number of activities is obvious. Two factors seem to interfere with this development – fear and professional jealousy. On the one hand there is concern about over-work, skill and accountability and on the other undue regard for professional qualifications rather than the ability to perform the task. Clinical managers seeking to rearrange working practices must be aware not only of the legal contract between the organization and the individual but also the pyschological contract, the set of expectations the employer and employee have of each other. This non-explicit contract may well be viewed differently particularly at times of change. The employee may feel exploited; the employer may sense stubbornness or lack of cooperation. Handled badly, significant problems can arise. Before introducing changes of this sort the ground should be well prepared. Job enhancement for one can lead to concentration on more relevant work for the other to the advantage of both and more importantly to the patients. Improvement in the quality of care should be the motivating factor. The financial gain from these changes may be real but it should be secondary to real improvements in quality.

A TEAM OF TEAMS   The purpose of clinical management teams is to make the best use of available resources to provide high quality care for individual patients and groups of patients. The team will exist in a hierarchical management structure. The management chart defines the organization in terms of authority, role and responsibility. The information and communication pathways up and down the organization can easily be identified. Action within discrete departments and specialty groups can be ordered and monitored; it is manageable. The organization chart shows how the workplace is organized and managed to get things done. Since the objective is to provide high quality care, the hospital management structure is therefore the hospital's quality management structure.

Patient care, however, rarely falls within any single management domain. A patient may need diagnostic services from pathology and radiology, treatment from different specialty doctors, nurses, physiotherapists and occupational therapists who in turn may need medical equipment maintained by medical physics and site management. Long established customs and practice have produced firm barriers and strong hierarchies and as the process of care moves amongst the vertical lines of accountability many boundaries have to be crossed. It is usually at these points that the system is at its weakest and the quality of care suffers. It is then too easy to blame people in another team for not delivering what is required.

Quality of services to patients depends on all staff in the organization providing a quality service to each other as well as to the patient. The challenge for clinical managers having built and shaped their team is to generate the understanding that the organization is a team of teams and to improve quality of care by helping to remove the organizational constraints that prevent people from doing their best. This involves a management approach which focuses on the objectives listed in Box 4.6.

Box 4.6
Improving quality of services

- ◆ Searching for and facilitating good practice.

- ◆ Foreseeing and eliminating barriers between staff groups.

- ◆ Identifying the requirements of the internal and external customer.

- ◆ Building teams that value every member's contribution.

- ◆ Improving quality by searching for faults in the system rather than finding people to blame.

- ◆ Involving staff at all levels in identification, analysis and solving of problems related to improving quality.

- ◆ Continually improving processes to eliminate problems.

Improving processes within single specialties or services, vertical parts of the organization, is a fairly straightforward management task. Improving processes across the organization requires much greater effort; the coordination of activities of members of a number of different teams. These people constitute an invisible multidisciplinary team composed of medics, nurses, paramedics, ancillary staff and managers whose members do not always know each other and do not always recognize that they are players on the same side. This team and its individual members needs to be identified. The processes that they operate need to be described and understood. Only then can faults in the system be identified and steps taken to remedy defects.

Experience has taught that knowledge of the system is held by the groups involved in the delivery of the process. Status does not provide knowledge of the process; working in it does. Multidisciplinary teams brought together in this way to solve specific problems are sometimes referred to as quality development teams. Clinical managers and their senior colleagues must show willingness and be able to work in such teams and recognize the contribution of others as being equal to their own. It is unlikely that problems will ever be solved on the basis that 'I am right because I am a surgeon' or 'you are wrong because you are a medical records officer'.

Working in such teams soon leads to the recognition that it is nearly always processes rather than people that let the system down. Properly established such teams can allow an analysis of problems in an atmosphere free from blame and members can be encouraged in a continual search for ways of improving the service.

Such teams can lead to significant improvements if they have:

♦ A thorough understanding of how the complex processes work.
♦ Knowledge of the improvement options available.
♦ Authority to implement agreed solutions.
♦ Support of staff to implement the agreed solutions.

Clinical managers will need to develop the skills necessary to recognize process issues, assemble the appropriate teams and take a lead in the breaking down of professional barriers. They must be able to will the means as well as the ends and then to monitor the outcomes.

SELF-MANAGEMENT   Both clinicians and managers have full timetables and frequently face difficult problems. For the clinician manager the pressures are significantly increased. Pressure can be a cause of good performance. Working for short periods to reach targets in a limited time can focus and channel activity in a rewarding way. Too much pressure, however, sustained over long periods, produces stress and poor performance.

Nothing is easier than being busy and for many, being busy seems to be an end in itself. Being effective is more difficult and requires planning and organization.

In the course of their work, medical managers frequently encounter a number of problems which interfere with their effectiveness. These include role conflict, lack of time, facing difficult decisions and frustration. It is difficult to deal with these problems adequately without a clear understanding of your own values, priorities and use of time.

Values   Values are an expression of your own needs; what you really want to achieve. What for you is the best balance of family life, work, intellectual needs and leisure interests. You will need to examine whether your life overall is arranged to allow you to move towards these goals.

In particular at work have you voluntarily or unwittingly taken on too much? Do you have realistic and clear goals against which you can assess your own performance? Are these goals and the decisions that you take consistent with your own ethical standpoint? Can you reconcile your duties as a doctor and a manager, and your work with your life outside? Dealing with these issues is not easy but the rewards in terms of stress reduction are high.

Priorities   It is clearly desirable to arrange work in such a way as to concentrate on essential activities rather than on trivia. Essential activities should be classified as important or urgent and the trivial work should be discarded. The essential work can then be further categorized as in Box 4.7.

Box 4.7
Prioritizing work

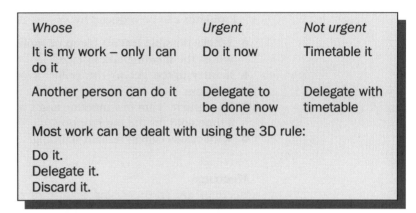

Whose	Urgent	Not urgent
It is my work – only I can do it	Do it now	Timetable it
Another person can do it	Delegate to be done now	Delegate with timetable

Most work can be dealt with using the 3D rule:

Do it.
Delegate it.
Discard it.

Do not be deceived into thinking something is urgent simply because it was transmitted to you by fax or over your mobile phone. If you have problems with discarding work put it in a dump file and then discard it six months later when you discover that you have never needed to resurrect it.

Most problems arise with larger projects, work which is essential but not urgent. It is all too easy to defer this work but fail to timetable it. Eventually it needs to be reclassified as work which is essential and urgent, commanding such high priority that large amounts of other urgent work must be displaced. This problem can only be avoided by timetabling the work when it is accepted.

Use of time   If you are an expert in time management you will have stopped reading this paragraph by now. If not you will at least recognize, as a clinician, that much of your time will be committed to activities such as clinics, ward rounds and operating sessions. Making the best use of your time will include not only using these fixed sessions to maximum advantage but also exercising control over the rest of your working day.

On your next train or plane journey buy a book on time management at the book stall and read it. Nearly all books of time management cover activities such as daily planning, keeping paperwork under control, managing interruptions and the value of meetings.

Common observation shows that clinicians are particularly poor at dealing with interruptions, meetings and saying no.

Interruptions

For many clinicians interruptions are merely requests to do their job; for example, to give clinical advice or attend at emergencies. Frequently, however, the telephone call or the 'drop-in' visit is neither urgent nor important. If a meeting is disrupted for a trivial call you may be wasting not only your own time but that of many of your colleagues who have taken the trouble to attend.

Problems can be reduced by:

♦ Where possible leave a bleep or mobile phone with a secretary whilst the meeting takes place.
♦ If interrupted get to the point, avoid small talk, identify the problem.
♦ Be explicit, 'I am in a meeting and I will phone you back', or set a time limit for the interruption.
♦ With casual callers remain standing.

Meetings

Meetings are an increasing feature of medical life. As a clinician manager you will be invited to many and feel almost obliged to attend. It is likely that there will be a mass of paperwork to wade through beforehand and in all probability it will arrive too late to allow you to do so. Consider whether your time at the meeting will be well spent. There are many reasons why people attend meetings including social reasons, the need to give or gather information and decision taking. If the meeting is likely to satisfy one of your personal objectives you should attend. If it is unlikely to do this and your presence is not essential to others your time will be better spent elsewhere.

Saying no

Many colleagues, in part because of their motivation and in part because of habit inculcated through years of being a junior doctor, find it difficult to say no. Some have become overly dependent on the goodwill and approval of others. Some seem simply to have lost the ability to distinguish between what is possible and what is impossible and to say no to unreasonable demands upon themselves or their team. The result is that inappropriate work is undertaken at the expense of performance of relevant tasks with consequent reduced satisfaction and demotivation.

Someone who is effective at self-management will:

♦ Feel in control of themselves and their work.
♦ Set high but realistic standards.
♦ Work to agreed and realistic deadlines.
♦ Delegate effectively.
♦ Confront difficult issues without procrastination.
♦ Learn when to say no.

♦ Balance work, family and leisure.
♦ Accept occasional failure and learn from it without inappropriate stress or demoralization.

CONCLUSION   The greatest asset of the NHS is the people who work in it. They come from a wide variety of backgrounds and cultures and bring with them a wide variety of skills, knowledge and attributes. There is a great variation of religious beliefs and ethical standpoints, of aspiration and motivation. People have different needs in terms of hours of work and recognition for work done. Most still value the NHS and want it to succeed. The turmoil of all the recent changes has led to some demoralization and many, even at fairly senior level, seem unclear as to the future.

Against this background there is a desperate need for good clinical leaders who can tap this huge resource of people, break down barriers and eliminate outdated and dysfunctional practices. Managers who can lead and develop teams and then go on to work with other managers to produce a fully participative team culture.

In my view such leaders will need time, resources and information. In addition, they must have credibility and this is most likely to arise from continuing in clinical activity; from feeling 'the heat of the kitchen'. Above all they must demonstrate the three key attributes of vision, trust and communication.

SUMMARY

In order to achieve the best results a manager should:

♦ Understand the task.
♦ Know and be able to communicate with the members of the team.
♦ Recognize and use appropriately an individual's skills.
♦ Identify and deal with dysfunctional behaviour.
♦ Motivate and reward the team.
♦ Understand that organizational quality is founded on personal quality.
♦ Demonstrate the three key attributes of vision, trust and communication.

FURTHER READING

> ♦ Turrel, T. (1993), *Transforming Doctors' Dilemmas*, Turrel, Thirsk.
>
> This book is a management development manual for doctors and their managerial colleagues and it is based on a study commissioned by the NHS Management Executive to identify those behavioural characteristics which distinguished excellent doctors in management.
>
> ♦ Handy, C. (1989), *The Age of Unreason*, Business Books, London.
>
> This very readable book not only demonstrates the inevitability of change, often occurring in ways that seem to be quite unexpected, but shows how it is possible to harness these changes for our advantage. It shows how to respond when 'the only prediction that will hold is that no predictions will hold'.
>
> ♦ Kakabadse, A., Ludlow, R. and Vinnicombe, S. (1988), *Working in Organisations*, Penguin, London.
>
> A well researched and thorough book using a case history format explaining the often complex relationships between people, their jobs and the organization.
>
> ♦ The Poems of Christina Rossetti (1830–94).
>
> For their sheer lyrical beauty. There's more to life than work.

REFERENCES

Belbin, R. (1981), *Management Teams – Why They Succeed or Fail.* Oxford: Butterworth/Heinemann.

Edgell, C. (1994), Eeney Meeny Miney Mo. *British Medical Journal* 3086–7.

Handy, C. (1985), *Understanding Organisations.* Aylesbury: Penguin.

Harwood, A. and Beauford, J. I. (1993), *Managing Clinical Services, a consensus statement.* London: IHSM.

Heirs, B. (1989), *The Professional Decision Thinker.* London: Grafton.

Herzberg, F. (1966), *Work and the Nature of Man.* London: World Publishing Company.

McGregor, D. (1966), *Leadership and Motivation.* London: MIT Press.

Nadler, D. and Tushman, M. L. (1980), *A Model for Diagnosing Organisation Behaviour. Organisation Dynamics.* Chicago: AMA.

Turrel, T. (1993), *Transforming Doctors' Dilemmas.* Thirsk: Turrel.

MANAGING WITHIN THE ORGANIZATION

Jenny Cowpe

Jenny Cowpe

OBJECTIVES

- ◆ To identify the key factors within the operation of an organization which determine the level of success it enjoys.

- ◆ To show how effective management structures and communication systems are essential for that success.

- ◆ To provide practical guidance on the contribution of clinical managers to corporate strategy and operations management.

INTRODUCTION

Most of us want our organizations to survive and prosper, yet few give any serious thought to how these aims should be achieved. To succeed in today's healthcare environment means to become truly competitive; to become competitive requires you, and your organization, to understand how to satisfy patients and purchasers – your customers – and to be committed to providing excellent service (Pearson, 1992). Turning your organization into a successful competitor, however, is not always easy. This chapter suggests how you can achieve this objective by examining:

- ◆ How organizations work.
- ◆ Effective management structures and communications systems.
- ◆ How to create a corporate strategy.
- ◆ Operations management.

Each section of this chapter outlines the main management concepts, applies them to the health service, describes the keys to success and highlights important issues for clinicians.

HOW ORGANIZATIONS WORK

Key management concepts

An organization's effectiveness in delivering its services or products is determined largely by the way its people behave. This behaviour reflects the way work is organized, authority is exercised and people are rewarded, which in turn are determined by the basic values, beliefs and assumptions which the organization holds. These values and beliefs derive from the organization's history, traditions and the work it does. They were originally shaped by its founders but subsequently have been influenced strongly by the dominant groups throughout the organization's existence (Handy, 1987).

Taken together, values and beliefs, and the resulting organizational structures and systems, give each organization its unique character or 'personality', which management writers usually describe as an organization's 'culture'. This is similar to the concept of national cultures and, in the same way, describes the essence of what makes one organization different from another and why each operates as it does. Put more simply, an organization's culture can be described as 'the way we do things around here'.

Thus all organizations have a culture, some stronger than others. But while all organizations have cultures of one kind or another, the key to success lies in having an appropriate culture – in other words, one which enables the organization to address current challenges. The survivors, and winners, are those organizations which can successfully adapt their beliefs and values, and their organizational structures and systems, to new tasks and challenges (Handy, 1987).

Your organization needs to be in this category!

The health service context

The concept of organizational culture applies as much to the health service as to commerce and industry, and is equally influential in shaping behaviour and productivity. In the health context, the 'culture' of a teaching hospital will be different from that of a community Trust, which will be different again from an acute general hospital, reflecting differences in their work and different patterns of delivery. Health service culture has been dominated traditionally (and not surprisingly) by the values of the clinical professions, particularly medicine and nursing, which emphasize individual patient care and high standards of practice but have had relatively little interest in costs.

In the last decade, however, new challenges have arisen, including:

◆ Changes in the social and economic environment: a rising demand for health care, the reduced availability of financial resources, greater consumer expectation based on knowledge of advances in medical technology.
◆ Introduction of the NHS internal market.
◆ Changes in NHS funding arrangements: the new weighted

capitation formula and the shift of investment from acute to primary and community care.

♦ New emphases in health policy: Health of the Nation targets, emphasis on outcomes and health gain, Patient's Charter and quality initiatives.

♦ Radical developments in working practices, such as the introduction of day case surgery.

As a result, new values have emerged, which stress responsiveness to patient demand, value for money and the importance of the whole organization delivering the right service, at the right time, at the right price. Although some tensions have developed between the 'old' values and the 'new' culture, most healthcare organizations now realize that to survive they must harness both high professional standards and realistic managerial goals.

Factors for success   To succeed in the complex environment of the 'new' National Health Service, healthcare organizations need to create cultures which:

♦ Foster an entrepreneurial approach, focusing on satisfying customers' needs (ahead of the competition) and identifying opportunities to create new business.

♦ Accept risk-taking in order to create new opportunities and welcome change as an opportunity, not a threat.

♦ Foster market and consumer awareness throughout the organization and aim for high levels of quality and service.

♦ Promote and provide education and training for all their staff and a supportive, open psychological environment which encourages employee participation and promotes initiative and a sense of responsibility at every level.

♦ Stress teamwork.

♦ Are tolerant of unconventional types of people and encourage creative ways of doing things.

♦ Believe in integrity and fair dealing with employees, suppliers and customers.

♦ Emphasize results rather than process (Barham, Fraser and Heath, 1986).

If these beliefs and values can be fostered, an organization will have a progressive, competitive culture, in which people are not only aware of the aims of the business, understand them and have the freedom to take initiatives, but are also personally involved in and committed to their achievement. Your organization needs to develop these key 'cultural' factors for success. If, like most, you need to change or reorientate your current culture, this can be achieved by creating a corporate strategy, developing an effective management structure and communications system and restructuring your operations.

Issues for clinical directors

Clinical directors need to:

◆ Understand the current corporate 'culture' of their organization.
◆ Be aware of, and understand, the external and internal challenges facing their organization.
◆ Decide with their chief executive, director of operations, and fellow clinical managers, which values and beliefs, structures and systems require changing to meet the new challenges.
◆ Agree and implement an appropriate action plan.

EFFECTIVE MANAGEMENT STRUCTURES AND COMMUNICATION SYSTEMS

Key management concepts

In order to deliver their services or products effectively, organizations need an appropriate management structure to ensure the efficiency of the basic operation, provide the environment for innovation and enable the organization to adapt to major threats and changes in its environment (Peters and Waterman, 1982).

An organization's management structure consists of a number of elements, including the basic design of the organization (which is usually developed on the basis of function, product/service or geographical location); the management arrangements and job structures; and the organization's systems, which link the component parts.

If we use an anatomical analogy and compare an organization to the human body:

◆ The skeleton is the basic design.
◆ The muscles are the management arrangements and jobs.
◆ The blood and guts are the staff.
◆ The body's systems (for example, the nervous system) are the organization's systems which flow through and link the different parts.

When considering the organization's design, the two basic principles are: firstly, that the design must be appropriate for the function of the organization, that is, 'form follows function'. For example, the design that is appropriate for an acute hospital, where services are concentrated, will be different from that which is right for a community Trust, which delivers services in many locations. Secondly, the design must be appropriate for the organization's culture, that is, the two must be in harmony, or frustration and ineffectiveness will result.

In considering the basic design, the 'designer' must decide on the primary division, that is between a structure based on function, e.g. sales/marketing, medical staff/nursing staff; on product, e.g. cars/trucks, cardiology/orthopaedics; or on location, e.g UK/Europe, different sites within a Trust. In addition, there is a further choice of whether to have a centralized or decentralized structure. Many organizations choose a decentralized system in order to encourage staff participation; if this is done, there must be a balance between corporate goals and the aims and activities of individual divisions within the organization, in order to achieve efficiency and meet output requirements.

As a separate consideration, management arrangements define the posts which will manage the whole and parts of the organization, the job content of these posts and the integrating mechanisms – that is, committee structures and rules and procedures which glue the organization together. To be effective in today's environment management arrangements must be simple, with clear lines of accountability, and there must be easily understood differentiation between management levels in the organization. Arrangements should also allow for appropriate customer involvement. Job descriptions must be unambiguous and allow scope for staff to control their work and participate in decisions and there should be a minimum of standing committees and rules, and an emphasis on flexibility and innovation.

Organizational systems, as indicated earlier, are concerned with flows or processes through the structure and should be designed to keep the organization moving, not to slow it up! Examples of organizational systems are budgetary systems, management information systems and communications systems. Taking communications systems as an example, the main principles of effective design to remember are that we never communicate as effectively as we think we do (any doctor who works in a busy outpatient clinic will testify to this fact!); furthermore, communication systems operate at two levels: i.e. the formal communication network (for example: committees, news bulletins, memoranda and letters) and the informal network between colleagues, friends or allies, which cuts across organizational boundaries and is often faster and more powerful than the formal system. When designing formal communication systems it is important to design more than one communications network, to encourage two-way rather than one-way communication (i.e. allow for feedback) to keep the linkages in the communication chain as few as possible and to make sure formal communication is regular, comprehensive and clear to the recipients.

Management structures   The design principles outlined above apply as much to healthcare organizations as to those in the commercial and industrial sectors. In the health service, however, a further major factor is the involvement of clinicians in management and we will now examine some effective models of healthcare management structures based on the principles set out above.

In acute care organizations, the best known structure for clinical management in the United Kingdom is that based on the Johns Hopkins 'directorate' model. This is an example of a structure based on 'product' and comprises:

♦ Clinical directorates based on either individual specialties or groups of specialties. In smaller organizations it is usual for the major specialties to become individual clinical directorates; in larger organizations there has been an increasing tendency to aggregate specialties and appoint a clinical head, with directors for each specialty within the larger grouping.

♦ Leadership provided by a multidisciplinary clinical management team comprising as a basic model

Either	*Or*
Clinical director	Clinical director
+	+
Business manager	Directorate general manager
+	
Nurse manager	

♦ Dedicated support from a human resources adviser and finance officer and (in some cases) an information manager.

♦ Corporate involvement of clinical directors in an organization-wide management board/executive committee.

Figures 5.1 and 5.2 show examples of clinical directorate systems in operation.

In our own hospital, the organizational structure based on a directorate system has proved effective because:

♦ It is simple.

♦ There is maximum delegation of authority to clinical directors and their teams.

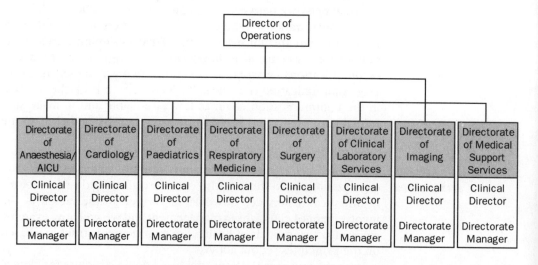

Figure 5.1
Royal Brompton Hospital: Clinical directorate structure

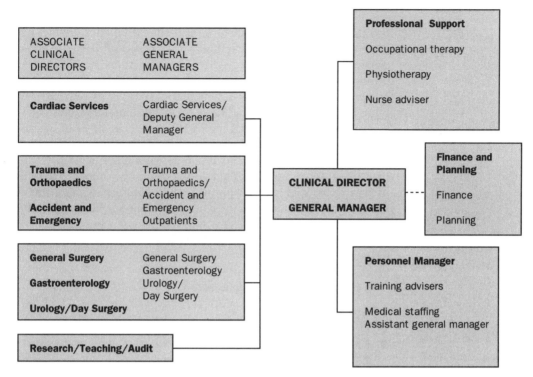

Figure 5.2
United Bristol Healthcare NHS Trust: Directorate of Surgery

♦ There is strong general management support both within the directorates, and from above, via the chief executive and director of operations.
♦ The director of operations coordinates directorate activities to ensure corporate goals are achieved.

A further development of this model, already introduced at Royal Brompton and currently being tested in a number of sites, is the 'internal purchaser/provider split', whereby clinical directorates are divided into 'purchasers' (i.e. the bed-holding clinical directorates) and 'providers' (typically the service clinical directorates such as radiology, pathology and medical support services). In this model, the budgets of the service directorates (or the non-pay elements of them) are devolved to the 'purchaser' clinical directorates, who 'contract' annually to purchase an agreed volume and mix of service. The aim of this development is to further sharpen the effective use of resources, by allowing clinicians to question their use of e.g. pathology services, with the incentive that an agreed proportion of the savings made will accrue to their directorate.

In addition, the clinical directorate structure can also be used to facilitate other functions, such as research and education in teaching hospitals. For instance, in the latest development at Royal Brompton, research coordinators and education coordinators have been appointed within each directorate, responsible to the clinical director, to pull together all activities under these headings and to provide an interface with the National Heart and Lung Institute (the postgraduate institute with which the Trust is associated). This pilot shows that a robust basic management structure can be adapted to other purposes, provided that clear lines of accountability are maintained and roles carefully defined.

In community Trusts, and those providing services for mental health and for people with a learning disability, there are a variety of organizational models. Although some community organizations have attempted to adapt the acute clinical directorate model, most are developing structures to suit their own circumstances. In particular, models based on dividing the organization on a locality basis are increasingly common. An example of this model from Premier Health is shown in Figure 5.3.

In the Premier Health structure:

◆ The design is based on localities, not products.
◆ Trust directors are also general managers of the localities.
◆ A key feature behind the design was the need and desire to involve general practitioners in the Trust's decision-making process, in an area where the majority of practices are fund-holding. Thus, with their agreement, general practitioners are represented on all the locality management teams, where they are in direct contact with the general manager (not junior staff), and can influence the major decisions taken. A major tenet for Trust staff is 'Premier Health works for general practitioners'.

Factors for success   Among the major factors influencing the effectiveness of health service management structures is the recognition that 'form follows function' as discussed earlier. This is illustrated in the three examples above, where the acute trusts are organized on product lines, and the community trust on a locality basis, to ensure the effective delivery of what purchasers most want, i.e. specific products on the one hand and comprehensive local care on the other. In addition, they succeed because the management structure is appropriate for the culture. In the cases illustrated, the organizations believe in devolving considerable management responsibility to clinical or locality groups, and value and encourage staff participation in making decisions.

For the clinical directorate model, other important success factors are:

◆ Choosing the appropriate number and size of the directorates. Reference has already been made to the growing tendency in larger organizations to amalgamate clinical directorates into larger units. There are trade-offs at work here between maxi-

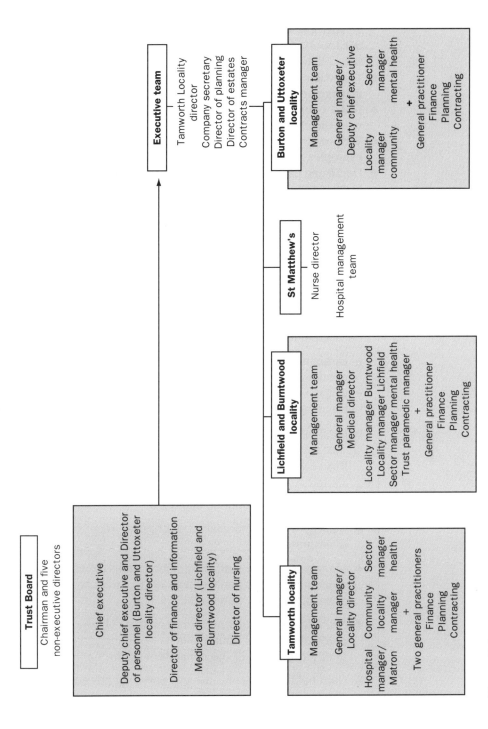

Trust Board
Chairman and five
non-executive directors

Chief executive

Deputy chief executive and Director
of personnel (Burton and Uttoxeter
locality director)

Director of finance and information

Medical director (Lichfield and
Burntwood locality)

Director of nursing

Executive team

Tamworth Locality
director
Company secretary
Director of planning
Director of estates
Contracts manager

Tamworth locality

Management team

General manager/
Locality director

Hospital   Community   Sector
manager/   locality   manager
Matron   manager   health
+
Two general practitioners
Finance
Planning
Contracting

**Lichfield and Burntwood
locality**

Management team

General manager
Medical director

Locality manager Burntwood
Locality manager Lichfield
Sector manager mental health
Trust paramedic manager
+
General practitioner
Finance
Planning
Contracting

St Matthew's

Nurse director

Hospital management
team

**Burton and Uttoxeter
locality**

Management team

General manager/
Deputy chief executive

Locality   Sector
manager   manager
community   mental health
+
General practitioner
Finance
Planning
Contracting

Figure 5.3
Premier Health management structure

mum representation of clinical staff in management and the size of management boards which involve all clinical directors. Smaller clinical directorates are easier for clinicians to manage but too many clinical directorates hinder cross communication and collaboration.

◆ The willingness of medical and clinical staff to participate in management.

◆ Good communications, both between clinical directorates and with the chief executive and senior managers.

◆ Well defined roles for management team members. Some examples are shown in Boxes 5.1, 5.2, and 5.3

◆ Dedicated professional accountancy and human resource advice for the management teams.

◆ The availability and viability of information systems to support decision-making by clinical management teams. In the Consensus Statement Survey undertaken in 1993, involving the British Medical Association (BMA) and Royal College of Nursing (RCN)

Box 5.1
Role of a clinical
director

The clinical director usually reports to the director of operations or chief executive.
   Principal responsibilities include:

◆ Directing the services of the clinical directorate, to ensure a high standard of clinical care and, where appropriate, due emphasis on research, development and teaching.

◆ Leading the clinical management team and representing the clinical directorate at the corporate management level.

◆ Developing the clinical directorate's business plan and monitoring performance against it.

◆ Managing the financial and physical resources of the directorate.

◆ Managing all the staff (in practice, management of non-medical staff is usually delegated to the nurse and business/directorate managers).

◆ Leading on quality standards and control, which includes medical audit, although this is commonly delegated to another member of the consultant staff.

◆ Nominating representatives to serve on Advisory Appointments Committees.

◆ Being responsible for the research and education coordinators, where appointed.

Royal Brompton, internal
document, 1994

Box 5.2
Role of a directorate
manager

The directorate manager reports to the clinical director. Principal responsibilities include:

◆ Acting as a full member of the clinical management team, sharing corporate responsibility with the clinical director for managing the services provided.

◆ Deputizing for the clinical director as required.

◆ Managing the clinical directorate's services on an operational basis including:
  – managing all staff (except medical staff) within the clinical directorate,
  – planning and managing the budget on behalf of the director,
  – developing the business plan for the clinical directorate and agreeing annual service contracts with other purchaser or provider clinical directorates.

◆ Marketing the clinical directorate's services and participating in the negotiation of contracts.

◆ Monitoring and managing all contracts on behalf of the director to ensure target output is achieved and quality standards are maintained.

◆ Managing the physical facilities and equipment to ensure that the clinical directorate acts in accordance with statutory requirements and Trust policies, e.g. fire, health and safety and COSHH (Control of Substances Hazardous to Health).

◆ Ensuring effective communication and liaison with other clinical directorates.

NB In some structures, the terms 'directorate manager' and 'business manager' are interchangeable. In others, the directorate manager role has replaced the two roles of business manager and nurse manager.

Where two roles remain, the business manager's staff management role is greatly reduced since the nurse manager is responsible for nursing staff. He/she will also share other responsibilities with the business manager, e.g. budget management, the development of the business plan and health and safety issues.

Royal Brompton, internal
document, 1994

amongst others, the quality of information systems was almost universally regarded as inadequate, both in terms of its fitness for the purpose and its reliability (British Association of Medical Managers (BAMM) *et al.*, 1993). This is a key issue still to be addressed by the majority of healthcare organizations.

Box 5.3
Role of a nurse
manager/senior nurse

The nurse manager/senior nurse is managerially account-able to the clinical director or to the business/directorate manager, depending upon the structure of the clinical management team.
　　Principal responsibilities include:

♦ Acting as a full member of the clinical management team, sharing corporate responsibility with the clinical director and business manager for managing services.

♦ Operational management of nursing staff.

♦ Managing the nursing budget and facilitating devolution of budgets to ward level.

♦ Participating in the preparation of the clinical director-ate's business plan and input to strategic planning.

♦ Participating in monitoring and managing contracts.

♦ Ensuring that agreed nursing standards of care and ser-vice are provided and all statutory requirements are ful-filled.

♦ Taking responsibility for nursing quality initiatives and monitoring professional standards.

♦ Providing professional advice for the clinical directorate and other healthcare professional staff.

♦ Ensuring the appropriate education, training and pro-fessional development of all nursing staff.

Royal Brompton, internal
document, 1994

♦ Facilitating nursing research.

Communications systems

As with management structures, the general principles outlined above about communications systems also apply in the health service.
　　To be effective, communications systems should:

♦ Address both internal and external audiences.
♦ Ensure that internal audiences include all staff in the organiza-tion and volunteers.
♦ Provide clear messages, e.g. about the organization as a caring/forward-looking, quality service organization.
♦ Use a variety of mechanisms to convey appropriate messages (Royal Brompton communications strategy, 1994, Box 5.4).

External communications are one of the key components in competitive success (Pearson, 1992); the subject is not discussed

Box 5.4
Royal Brompton's
internal
communications
system

Written
Quarterly publication (staff and external audiences).
Monthly news bulletin (for staff).
Payslip letters by chairman/chief executive.
Open letters/mailshots from chief executive.
Regular directorate/departmental news bulletins.

Oral
Open meetings chaired by chief executive on a regular basis.
Team briefing.
Heads of department meetings.
Open meetings within directorates.
Open door policy by all senior staff.
Courteous response to requests for information by all switchboard and reception staff.

Visual
Walking the shop floor by senior staff.
Use of notice boards for information/press coverage/event publicity.
Exhibitions in foyers.
Use of videos for staff induction and education.
Monitoring improvements to physical environment.

Behavioural
Smart professional appearance.
Uniforms for front line staff with patient contact.
Wearing of badges in approved house style.

here, however, because this chapter is concerned with managing within the organization.

Key factors for a successful communications system include strong commitment to open communications by the chief executive and senior management team, a management structure which facilitates the easy passage of two-way communications, a multi-faceted communications system, i.e. written, oral and visual channels and ideally, regular 'communications audits' to see how well you are doing!

Issues for clinical directors

Key issues for clinicians participating in management are:

◆ Time to participate.
◆ Knowledge base: clinicians need to acquire management knowledge quickly and require some training in management skills.
◆ Tensions between the requirements of the managerial and clinical roles (this will be particularly acute at times of crisis, when conflicts of interest may arise).

♦ Relationships with senior general managers such as the chief executive and director of operations. Their support for the clinician manager role is crucial in making it effective.

♦ Genuine and effective delegation of authority to take decisions and to act, including control of staff, budgets and facilities and input into business planning.

♦ Effective involvement in corporate decision-making processes, including strategic planning and corporate strategy.

♦ Communications: clinical directors need to appreciate how communication systems work outside medicine and the importance of ensuring that information is passed to all staff.

♦ Incentives (why bother?)

CREATING A CORPORATE STRATEGY

Key management concepts

To survive and prosper, an organization needs a corporate strategy. This is a statement of long-term objectives, which define the direction an organization will take over the next few years. The purpose of a corporate strategy is to set a clear strategic direction, concentrate everyone's efforts and ensure that all major decisions taken are consistent with the long-term objectives.

A clear direction is the crucial ingredient of corporate strategy; without it there will be no concentration of effort by staff or consistency in either decision-taking or major investment. Organizations which lack direction will underperform and in the long run probably not survive. President Kennedy's famous target – 'to put a man on the moon by the end of the decade' – was a simple expression of strategic direction which became the crucial foundation of America's strategy in the space race (Pearson, 1992).

An effective corporate strategy must be simple: huge efforts invested in finding and articulating the ultimate strategy to give your organization a 'sustainable competitive advantage' are likely to be a waste of time and resources, since there are too many major and minor shocks that influence strategic options which cannot possibly be anticipated (Waterman, 1989). In addition, the strategy must look forward at least five years (a corporate strategy is concerned with major changes and developments which take time to come to fruition), must address the broad context of the political, economic, social and technical environments in which the organization operates and must focus on the core issues. This can be done at two levels:

♦ Level 1: by concentrating on the identification of the five or six key decisions that an organization must get right in order to prosper over the following few years (Argenti, 1989).

♦ Level 2: by examining future policy for the major services and systems which are key parts of the organization.

To achieve successful implementation, a corporate strategy must be backed by projects and action plans to achieve the desired strategic goals; it must also gain the commitment of all the key players in the organization.

To produce a corporate strategy it is best to use a simple, straightforward conceptual process, i.e.

◆ Where are we now?
◆ Where do we want to be?
◆ How do we get there?
◆ Action.
◆ How are we doing?

Essentially the process consists of collecting data, study and evaluation of the options, and taking decisions (Argenti, 1989). The chief executive and his/her senior management team should lead the process, with input from key players whose commitment is essential to its success.

The health service context

The general principles of creating a corporate strategy are directly applicable to the health service. Health service organizations are now subject to rapid change, both in the general and healthcare environments. A corporate strategy which sets out a clear strategic direction is essential.

Like most other major corporations, the National Health Service has abandoned the heavily prescribed and analytical strategic planning process of the 1970s and 1980s, which was based on careful forecasting but was not delivering results. Instead, purchasers and providers are adopting simpler, more flexible and more realistic approaches to corporate strategy. A number of different approaches are used; described in Box 5.5 is an example of the directional planning system used at Royal Brompton, which has proved highly effective.

Factors for success

The directional planning process has been very well received by Royal Brompton staff. Its strengths are those which make any strategic planning process effective:

◆ *Simplicity*: the process is straightforward and easy to use.
◆ *Practicality*: it focuses on strategic objectives which can be quantified.
◆ *Deliverability*: it requires specific projects to be developed and timetabled.
◆ *Openness and commitment*: key staff are involved in the working groups (membership normally numbers from 6 to 10) and all staff can attend presentations and submit comments for consideration.

Box 5.5
Royal Brompton's
directional planning
process

♦ The aim of the directional planning process is to identify the overall strategic direction for the Trust and the strategic objectives for the Trust's major services and functions.

♦ Directional planning has four major components:
  - existing realities: an analysis of emerging trends, market pressures, environmental constraints,
  - issues: strengths and weaknesses within the organization, opportunities and threats both inside and outside the organization,
  - willed future: identification of the desired future in 5–7 years,
  - action plans: specific projects designed to achieve the willed future.

♦ Key features of the process include:
  - initial identification by the chief executive and senior managers of major topics for investigation,
  - the establishment of multidisciplinary working groups to examine each topic,
  - the production of short reports to be discussed by the executive group and at open meetings to which any member of staff can come,
  - final presentation to the Trust Board for approval.

William Bain, Royal
Brompton Hospital, internal
document, August 1991

Issues for clinical directors   As clinical directors, you will be involved in determining the corporate strategy for your organizations. You need to:

♦ Understand the major environmental influences (so far as they can be determined) which will affect your organization over the next few years

♦ Acquaint yourself fully with your organization's corporate strategic planning process (providing that there is one!)

♦ Decide your own views about the five or six issues which your organization must address in the next few years.

OPERATIONS MANAGEMENT

Key management concepts

Operations management is concerned with the efficient conversion of an organization's resources (manpower, materials and money) into the goods or services which the organization provides, in order to satisfy customer demand in terms of both quantity and quality. Thus the design, planning and control of the systems which produce these goods or services are key elements of operations management. Its principal objectives are customer satisfaction and resource productivity; as such, it is involved in a constant search for quality improvement and value for money expressed as:

♦ *Economy*: thrift and good housekeeping.
♦ *Efficiency*: ensuring that maximum useful output is gained from the resources input to each activity.
♦ *Effectiveness*: ensuring that outcome matches the predetermined objectives.

Strong operations management is crucial to an organization's long-term success. 'The greatest marketing plan in the world, coupled with strong financial management, will be wasted if a company can't make the right product at the right time and the right price, or if it can't deliver it to the right place day after day and month after month' (Kelly and Kelly, 1988). Operations management plans must be fully integrated with corporate strategy, because most organizations must live for a long time with their investment choices, e.g. major capital equipment, and, once a system is in place, it tends to dictate which new products or services the organization can easily consider in future (Kelly and Kelly, 1988).

Operations managers need a tool kit of techniques to be effective, including problem-solving and 'management of change' skills. Some problem-solving kits involve statistical techniques and probability theories; in reality, the majority of problems, particularly in the public sector, are amenable to common sense and logical analysis, as illustrated in Figure 5.4. When trying to improve any operation, there are seven major operations management systems that can be examined. These are shown in Box 5.6, which provides a useful checklist.

There are also a number of management philosophies to assist. Two which are gathering momentum currently are the management philosophy of Dr W. Edwards Deming, the American statistician credited with being the prime catalyst behind the revival of post-war Japanese industry, and the 1990s concept of business process re-engineering. Deming's philosophy stresses an obsession with quality, to 'delight the customer' not merely to satisfy him/her. Quality is achieved through analysing and streamlining the production process within an organization, with emphasis on a scientific approach to quality control. Business process re-engineering involves 'going back to the beginning and inventing a better way of doing work' because most Western industries are still structured on the basis of the division of labour principles set out by Adam Smith two hundred years ago, that is, we organize work by breaking it down into tasks which individual people perform, rather than looking at the overall process (Hamner and Champney, 1993). This approach therefore emphasizes the necessity of reorganizing the basic business processes in order to achieve dramatic improvements in performance, asking such questions as:

♦ Why do we do what we do?
♦ Why do we do it the way we do it?
♦ How can we deliver better value to the customer?

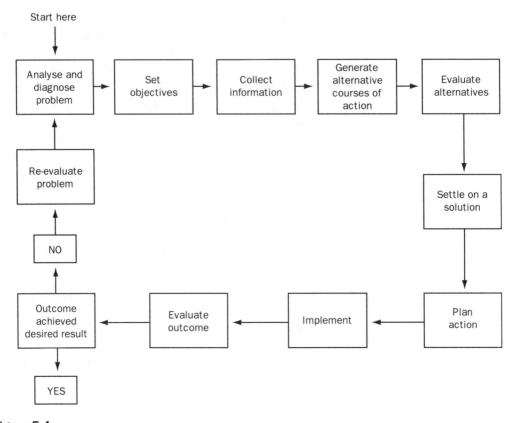

Figure 5.4
The problem-solving model
Source: Institute of Health Service Management (1983)

The major thrust of these philosophies is similar: that is, to achieve better performance it is necessary to rethink and redesign the processes by which services or products are delivered. Improvements to production systems, however, mean managing change effectively. A logical and sensitive process is required and a suggested sequence is shown in Figure 5.5 based on the ideas of Rosabeth Moss Kanter (Kanter, 1989).

The health service context   All the management concepts outlined above are applicable to the health service. In the NHS, operations management is concerned with the efficient management of all the resources required to deliver diagnosis, treatment and care to patients, as well as appropriate support to patients' relatives and carers, in both hospital and community. Operations management is concerned directly with the seven M's in Box 5.6.

The scope of operations management within the NHS varies, however, between provider organizations. At its fullest extent, in

Box 5.6
The seven M's of
operations
management

1. *Man- and womanpower.* Effective management of staff is a powerful tool to improve a system's function.

2. *Materials.* The materials used can greatly affect how a process should be designed, how swiftly and efficiently it runs, and what level of product quality can be achieved.

3. *Machines.* Choosing machines with the right (for your needs) size, speed, capacity, flexibility, reliability, features, and operational capabilities is a cornerstone of good operations management. Knowing when and how to incorporate new technology is an increasingly important factor in keeping an organization competitive and profitable.

4. *Managers.* The quality of managers – their training and experience, and their ability to motivate staff – is crucial to developing and maintaining a competitive edge.

5. *Messages.* Making sure the right information is communicated to the right people at the right time is also a cornerstone of a good production system.

6. *Methods.* There is usually more than one way of accomplishing required tasks. Choosing the best method for the job at hand is as important as selecting the most efficient machine or staff.

7. *Money.* Understanding the financial end of a production process and matching the system's financial needs to the organization's needs is necessary to keep the machines running and the business profitable.

Adapted from Kelly and
Kelly, 1988

Box 5.7
Operations
management in an
acute hospital

Services involved:

Clinical services

Clinical support services (e.g. pharmacy, therapy services, technical services)

Patient services (medical records, outpatient services, ward administrators)

Hotel services (catering, domestic services, laundry and linen, portering, security, telephones)

Estates services

Purchasing and supply services

The staff, budgets and facilities applicable to these services

Figure 5.5
The change
management cycle

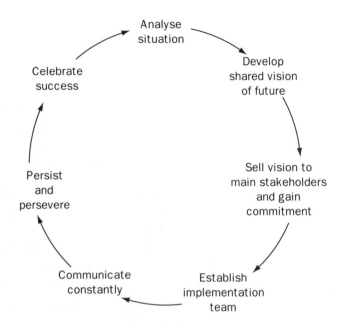

an acute hospital environment, it controls the whole 'production process' by managing services shown in Box 5.7. In this case, the operations management function is normally led by a director of operations, reporting directly to the chief executive. A typical management structure is shown in Figure 5.6.

In community and mental health trusts the same general definition of operations management applies, but the functions will be structured to suit the way the organizations operate.

Key issues on the current healthcare operations management agenda include:

♦ Streamlining the clinical 'production process'
   - restructuring clinical and support services to deliver cost-effective care (an example is shown below in Box 5.8)
   - reducing access and waiting times for treatment and care
   - reducing length of stay and cancellation of operations in hospitals
♦ Delivering a quality service
   - assessing consumer expectation and satisfaction
   - meeting Patient's Charter and local quality standards
   - introducing clinical audit and quality teams
   - meeting accreditation standards
♦ Improving labour productivity
   - improving motivation and productivity levels
   - undertaking grade and skill mix reviews and performance appraisal

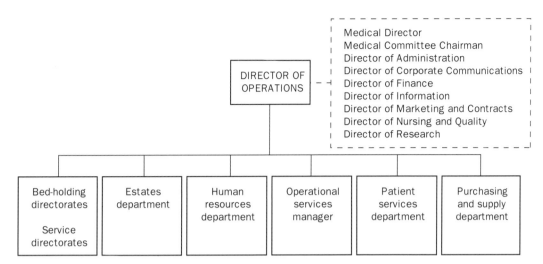

Figure 5.6
Royal Brompton hospital operations structure.
———, Direct managerial responsibility; – – – –, liaison.

- reviewing and restructuring pay and reward systems
- improving training and career planning, including Opportunity 2000
- rethinking communication systems
♦ 'Sweating' the estate assets
- improving asset utilization and productivity
- ensuring effective maintenance programmes and equipment replacement programmes
♦ Improving purchasing and supply systems
- enhancing value for money purchasing, involving clinical choice and product appraisal
- creating/maintaining good supplier relationships
♦ Controlling and reducing risks
- analysing risks: direct patient care risks, indirect patient care risks, health and safety risks, organizational risks
- creating a risk management strategy
- implementing risk control and risk reduction
♦ Tightening financial management
- improving costing systems and competitive pricing strategies
- controlling labour costs
- generating income
- ensuring tight budgetary control
♦ Improving management competence
- improving recruitment and selection (particularly of clinical directors), enhancing training and education programmes.

Box 5.8
An operational review

During 1992, in response to financial pressures, Royal Brompton undertook an operational review of both clinical and support services, conducted by external management consultants.

The purpose of this review was to identify operational improvements in quality, service and cost which could be made in the context of Royal Brompton's tripartite mission of clinical work, research and teaching.

The management consultants' report highlighted a number of deficiencies and discrepancies. It was proposed that Royal Brompton should create a better balance between planned activity and capacity by:

♦ Reducing staffing levels, changing skill mix and increasing activity in all clinical areas.
♦ Improving the patient process management by:
  – coordinating admissions,
  – aggregating wards,
  – flexing staffing,
  – appointing a Master Scheduler to schedule admissions and resources.

Target savings were given for each clinical directorate and clinical management teams were asked to develop their proposals in response to the report's findings. Plans were discussed and agreed by the chief executive and senior management team and implemented by the unit general manager and the clinical management teams. The whole process, from initial preparation and proposals to the final implementation, took three months.

As a result:

♦ Staffing levels were reduced by between 15 and 21% depending on professional group, resulting in large cost savings.
♦ Catheter laboratory and theatre schedules were radically reorganized, wards aggregated and a master scheduler appointed.
♦ The patient process was dramatically improved, with fewer delays, fewer cancellations (reduced from 25% to approximately 3%) and less time spent overall by the patient from initial referral, through diagnosis to completion of treatment.

Factors for success   In operations management success depends upon:

♦ Building a management structure and creating a management style which encourages staff participation in the decision-making process.

♦ Ensuring close integration between corporate strategy and operations management decisions. Service providers should be involved in the creation of corporate strategy, not simply be asked to react to predetermined strategic plans (Kelly and Kelly, 1988).

♦ Creating an understanding at all levels of the need to 'sweat all the assets' of the organization, i.e. manpower, materials and money.

♦ Developing good information systems. If relevant, timely and accurate information is not available, the organization is likely to function at a sub-optimal level, which will affect its long-term survival.

♦ Carefully selecting operations managers, including clinicians. Effective operations management demands a high level of analytical and interpersonal skills, sound judgement and sensitivity.

Issues for clinical   Operations management is the area where clinical directors are
directors   most active, as leaders or participants in clinical management teams.

Key issues for clinical directors involved in operations management include:

♦ Appropriate development and training opportunities. Training and development needs identified by clinical staff in the recent Consensus Statement document included:

financial management	change management
business management	audit management
information management	time management
marketing	appraisal skills
quality management	

(BAMM *et al.*, 1993)

♦ Availability of dedicated accountancy and human resource management support.

♦ Accurate, timely and relevant information on activity and performance against contract, manpower and income and expenditure.

♦ Effective communication between clinical directors and the director of operations and chief executive.

♦ Involvement in the development of corporate strategy, in business planning, and in negotiating and managing contracts with purchasers.

CONCLUSION   This chapter has examined the main issues involved in managing within the organization and has described how you can help to turn your own organization into a successful competitor. Clinical directors cannot undertake this task alone. Real and sustained progress is achieved only through effective teamwork between the clinical and managerial professions and by harnessing the skills of all the staff, thus gaining everyone's commitment to the achievement of excellent service.

Tomorrow's successful organizations will be those who can achieve these goals.

SUMMARY

The competitive nature of today's healthcare environment requires organizations to:

◆ Encourage an entrepreneurial culture, in which people look for new opportunities, accept risks and demand education and development.

◆ Create a corporate strategy in order to set a clear strategic direction, concentrate efforts, and ensure that all major decisions taken are consistent with the long-term objectives.

◆ Establish an effective management structure, which suits the organization's purpose and its culture, and encourages staff participation in management decisions.

◆ Ensure that the processes by which services are delivered are as cost effective as possible, while providing a quality of care to delight the customer.

FURTHER READING

◆ Deal, T. and Kennedy, A. (1988), *Corporate Cultures*, Penguin, London.

A useful exploration of corporate culture: easy to read.

◆ Handy, C. (1990), *The Age of Unreason*, Arrow, London.

A stimulating exploration of the nature and process of change and its impact on organizations as we approach the third millennium.

◆ McCormack, M. H. (1986), *What They Don't Teach You at Harvard Business School*, Fontana, London.

Practical advice for managers, designed to fill the gaps between theory and practice, based on day to day experience of running a business and managing people.

◆ Moss Kanter, R. (1984), *The Change Masters*, Unwin, London.

Essential reading for those who wish to understand how to initiate innovation within organizations to achieve corporate success.

♦ Peters, T. J. and Austin, N. (1986), *Passion for Excellence*, Fontana, London.

A sequel to the widely read *In Search of Excellence*, this book examines how to create and sustain superior performance over the long haul. A lengthy text, but well worth dipping into and absorbing the lessons.

♦ Senge, P. M. (1990), *The Fifth Discipline*, Doubleday, New York.

A fascinating exploration of 'the learning organization' which took North America by storm.

REFERENCES

Argenti, J. (1989), *Practical Corporate Planning*. London: Unwin.

Barham, K., Fraser, J. and Heath, L. (1986), *Management for the Future*. Ashridge Management College.

BAMM/BMA/IHSM/RCN (1993), *Managing Clinical Services*. London.

Hamner, M. and Champney, J. (1993), *Re-Engineering the Corporation*. New York: Harper.

Handy, C. (1987), *Understanding Organisations*. Harmondsworth, Middlesex: Penguin.

Kanter, R. M. (1989), *When Giants Learn to Dance. Mastering the Challenges of Strategy Management and Careers in the 1990s*. London: Routledge.

Kelly, F. J. and Kelly, H. M. (1988), *What They Really Teach You at the Harvard Business School*. London: Grafton Books.

Pearson, G. (1992), *The Competitive Organisation*. London: McGraw-Hill.

Peters, T. J. and Waterman, R. H. (1982), *In Search of Excellence: lessons from America's best-run companies*. London: Harper & Row.

Waterman, R. H. (1989), *The Renewal Factor*. Great Britain: Bantam.

MANAGING CONTRACTS

CHAPTER 6

Kim Hodgson

OBJECTIVES

♦ To explore the nature of contracting in the internal market of the NHS: its objectives, content and problems.

♦ To identify the contribution of the clinical manager to contracting in terms of preparation, leadership and negotiating skills.

INTRODUCTION

Contracting is a rapidly developing field in the NHS. It largely determines the resources which will be available for patient care and strongly influences which patients get care and which do not. For these reasons, contracting cannot be left entirely to non-clinicians. Making sure that contracts are right for you and right for your patients is one of the most important functions of the clinical director.

This chapter outlines the contracting process in the NHS internal market and highlights the role which clinical directors and other senior clinicians should play in the process.

The first part of the chapter explains how a market works and highlights the key differences between the *managed market* of the NHS and the sort of market in which commercial enterprises work.

This is followed by a discussion of the main players in the internal market – providers, purchasers and consumers. The chapter examines the *contract* as a formal agreement between purchasers and providers and outlines the content of a contract.

A number of important contracting issues are then covered: the appropriate units of measurement in health care, how to estimate activity levels in contracts and how to deal with quality and pricing.

Finally, the central role which clinical directors should have in the contracting process is highlighted and a brief outline of how to prepare for and conduct contract negotiations is given.

OFF TO MARKET!

A market is a place where people trade. Sellers offer the goods and services which they would like to sell and buyers purchase what they need. A market offers a mechanism through which both the needs of sellers and buyers can be met. A market works well when both parties are satisfied with the deal which has been struck.

At least in theory, a market should perform a number of functions:

♦ It should ensure that sellers or producers only make what people want to buy. The market forces producers to be *responsive* to the needs of customers.

♦ It should ensure that goods and services are produced efficiently and offered at the lowest possible price. Clearly, if producer A is able to offer the same service at a lower price than B, customers will start to buy from A instead of B. B will then have to find ways of reducing his price or will have to give up and go out of business. Only efficient producers should survive in a market.

♦ It should encourage innovation (Manning and Dunning, 1994). Customers are always on the lookout for new or better products and services. If a particular supplier can introduce a new product or a superior version of an existing product, again customers will switch their purchasing behaviour to the new provider, thus stimulating existing providers to innovate as well.

♦ It should match capacity to demand. If customers only want so many of a particular product, suppliers will have to reduce their capacity to that level or be left with unsaleable goods. Similarly, if demand exceeds supply, existing suppliers will increase their capacity or increase their prices and new suppliers will enter the market, attracted by the higher prices which are available.

To a large extent, these theoretical considerations work in practice. There are many examples from the marketing literature of market forces changing the behaviour of products to the benefit of customers. Companies which have introduced products which nobody wanted have had to withdraw them or go out of business, prices have been driven down by new competitors entering the market and a look around your own home will illustrate the amount of innovation stimulated by market forces.

All of these benefits, however, come from a *free market* and a free market has particular characteristics:

♦ The consumer has purchasing power which he or she can use freely – the consumer can decide where to spend his or her money.

♦ There are competing providers chasing consumers. Without competition in the market, none of the benefits will be realized. The absence of competing providers is called a *monopoly*.

♦ New providers can enter the market and unsuccessful providers are forced to leave it.

♦ The consumer has the *information* required to make rational choices between competitive offerings.

When the internal market in the National Health Service was established, the government hoped that the benefits of a free market would come to be realized in health care. In particular it was hoped that market mechanisms would:

◆ Increase efficiency and lower cost per unit of care.
◆ Encourage consumer (patient) choice.
◆ Stimulate innovation.

This strategy has to be seen in the context of a global problem. Everywhere in the world, demand for health care outstrips the ability of any economy to meet that demand. Demand is driven by public expectations, by medical innovation and by the changing characteristics of the population.

At the time of writing, the jury is still out on the extent to which the creation of an internal market and its associated reforms will deliver these benefits. There is some evidence of progress on driving up efficiency and stimulating innovation but the concept of increased patient choice remains notional.

There are, in practice, significant differences between the NHS internal market and the pure free market of economists:

◆ In many parts of the country, real competition within the NHS does not exist.
◆ Consumers (patients) do not decide what to buy and where to buy it. Purchasing decisions are taken on their behalf by health authorities, commissioning agencies and general practitioners. General practitioners take decisions on behalf of their patients either by directly commissioning, in the case of fundholding GPs, or through their referral patterns.
◆ Consumers, apart from those with private health insurance, do not decide how much should be spent on health care as opposed to other goods and services. The total funding of the NHS is a political judgement: it is a cash limited service.
◆ Suppliers cannot easily enter and leave the market. There are substantial barriers to the entry of new providers into the NHS and even to the extension of the roles of existing providers. There are also substantial political barriers which prevent unsuccessful suppliers from 'going to the wall'.
◆ Consumers still have only a very low level of the information with which to make informed choices.

The internal market of the NHS is *not* a free market – it is a *managed market*. In a managed market, market mechanisms are moderated by other processes such as political decision-making and the influence of strong professional groups.

Another important difference between the managed market of the NHS and a free market is the tension which exists between healthcare choices for *individuals* and healthcare choices for whole populations.

So how does the internal market work in practice?

There are three main players in the market.

Providers are any organizations which provide healthcare services. These include NHS Trusts and directly managed units (DMUs) but also include providers in the private and voluntary sectors.

Purchasers include any individual or body which is responsible for purchasing healthcare services for a particular group of people. The main purchasers in the NHS are commissioning agencies and fundholding GPs. Commissioning agencies are consortia of district health authorities which have agreed to work together to commission or purchase services for their populations. In the longer term, commissioning agencies will probably be replaced through full mergers of district health authorities and FHSAs will merge with DHAs. Purchasers could also include local authorities, other NHS Trusts, private companies and voluntary agencies.

Consumers are the members of the public who actually use healthcare services. We use the word consumer in preference to *patient* because there are areas of healthcare provision such as health education, maternity services and services for people with learning difficulties and so on which deal with individuals who are not ill.

CONTRACTING FOR CARE

In the NHS, health care is purchased not by the consumer but by a purchaser acting on behalf of a group of consumers. A health authority or commissioning agency purchases services for the residents of its area and a fundholding GP purchases services for patients registered with the practice. In most cases, services are purchased *in advance* of their being consumed – rather like making a block booking with a hotel. You do not know exactly who is going to stay but you know that you are likely to need 300 bedrooms.

The mechanism through which this purchase is made is a *contract* between the purchaser and the provider. Contracts within the NHS are like any other form of contract *except that they are not enforceable in law*. It is probable that the government was nervous about a series of court cases between its health authorities and its NHS Trusts – essentially one part of the state suing another.

Like any other contract, an NHS purchaser:provider contract will spell out:

♦ What services are to be provided.
♦ How much is to be provided.
♦ To what quality standard services are to be provided.
♦ When services are to be provided.

♦ How much will be paid for the services which are to be provided.

In addition, a contract may address questions such as:

♦ How will performance be monitored?
♦ What information will have to be provided as part of the contract?
♦ What happens if something goes wrong?

The contracting timetable   The contracting process in the NHS takes place to a timetable set by national government and is driven by the public spending round. Until the government decides how much is available to spend on the NHS, the process of contract negotiation cannot really start.
The key points in the timetable are shown in Box 6.1.

Box 6.1.
The contracting timetable

STAGE	TIME
Price procedures	May
Value for money market comparison	June/July
Preliminary purchasing plan	October
Service specification from purchaser	October
Consultation meetings	December/January
Contract negotiations	December/January/February
Firm purchasing plan	November/December
Formal proposals received	January
Negotiations concluded	March
Contracts signed	31 March

CONTRACTING FOR WHAT   When a purchaser places a contract with a provider, what exactly is the purchaser purchasing? How do we describe the goods and services which an NHS provider produces?

The terms in which we describe the goods and services of NHS providers are sometimes referred to as the *currency* of the system – the units of health care used in setting contracts and managing performance. At the moment, most units are measures of throughput or activity rather than outcome. Finished consultant episodes (FCEs) are currently the most common form of currency for acute care and contacts the most common form of currency for community care.

When the internal market started, the nature of the currency was largely defined by what our information systems could measure or attempt to measure (Raftery and Gibson, 1994). This tended to reflect the Körner system, a system of performance measurement established in the NHS on the recommendation of the Körner Commission in the late 1980s.

The main units of currency were:

◆ Finished consultant episodes (FCEs) also known as completed consultant episodes (CCEs).
◆ Surgical procedures.
◆ Outpatient attendances.
◆ Patient contacts.

A finished consultant episode referred to the care which took place from the point at which a given patient was admitted under the care of a named consultant to the point at which the patient was discharged *from the care of that consultant*.

Surgical procedures were relatively simple to define and not too difficult to count as were outpatient attendances.

Patient contacts applied primarily to community services and to the work of the professions allied to medicine such as physiotherapy.

At the start of the internal market, most contracts were based on *average specialty costs*. Under this system, a directorate such as general medicine would take its total costs and divide this by the number of finished consultant episodes. The result was the price that would be charged for a finished consultant episode in general medicine. Over time, average specialty costing, whilst having the virtue of simplicity, started to cause real problems. It only required a fairly small change in the mix of patients treated (case mix) for the price to become unrealistic. If, for example, we started to treat patients who needed to stay in hospital longer or who needed more expensive medication, the average specialty cost would no longer be a good way of setting price and the provider would find that not enough money was coming in to cover the costs of care. Box 6.2 shows how a change in case mix can lead to a shortfall in resources.

Increasingly, providers have sought to move away from average specialty costing and to quote prices for particular procedures or for particular types of patient usually defined by diagnosis. Much greater progress has been made in surgical specialties where it is easier to cost particular procedures than it is in non-surgical specialties.

Similarly, pricing in contracts is increasingly starting to differentiate between inpatient, day case and outpatient care and, for outpatients, between initial attendances and follow-up attendances.

Difficulties also arise when using contacts as a basis for pricing in community services and in the professions allied to medicine (PAMs). The problem is similar to that of average specialty costing. A contact could be anything from popping in to say hello to a patient in his or her own home through to carrying out a major

Box 6.2
Effect of change in
case mix

Procedure	Cost	Scenario 1 Volume	Scenario 2 Volume
Complex major	£5000	25	30
Major	£3000	25	30
Moderate	£1500	25	20
Minor	£500	25	20
		100	100
Average cost		£2500	£2800
Total cost		£250 000	£280 000
Total income		£250 000	£250 000
Effect		£ –	(£30 000)

nursing procedure. Only the ethics of the professionals involved prevent them from responding to the pressure to drive up 'efficiency' by doing more 'pop ins' and less real care delivery.

However much we refine these forms of measurement, we are still measuring *what we do* rather than what we *achieve*. Over the next five years or so, it is likely that there will be a steady move towards *commissioning for health gain*. In this model, the currency will be the benefits delivered in terms of the health state of the patient of client. Instead of commissioning a thousand hip replacements, commissioners will commission *programmes of care* which result in the achievement of agreed levels of mobility and freedom from pain.

A move towards commissioning for health gain will offer a number of significant advantages:

◆ It will encourage innovation in clinical practice both in terms of efficiency and effectiveness.
◆ It will tend to drive out interventions of doubtful efficacy – if you cannot show what it does commissioners are not going to buy it.
◆ It will promote integrated models of health care which bring together hospital-based and community-based elements of care.
◆ It will enable health promotion and disease prevention to be contracted for in the same way as curative medicine.
◆ It will be a better model for chronic conditions.

HOW MANY WOULD YOU LIKE?   Most contracts specify a *volume* of services to be provided. A Trust might be contracted to carry out 500 hip replacement procedures or to carry out 500 FCEs in general medicine.

Increasingly, contracts are differentiating between *emergency* and *elective* cases. Thus the contract might specify 400 emergency and 100 elective episodes of a particular sort.

Some contracts place *tolerances* around the contracted volumes. Thus a typical contract might specify 500 episodes *plus or minus* 5%. The tolerances are designed to allow for the difficulty in predicting patient flows with complete accuracy.

In agreeing volumes, the provider needs to be sure that the contracted volume for emergency work reflects the likely pattern of emergency admissions. If insufficient capacity for emergency work has been contracted, emergency admissions will keep displacing elective admissions leading to patient dissatisfaction, under-performance on the elective side of the contract and lengthening waiting lists.

The provider also needs to consider the impact of contracted elective volumes on waiting lists. If contracted capacity is less than required, waiting lists will lengthen which will make the provider unpopular with local GPs and their patients.

The contract should specify very clearly what happens when it becomes apparent that there will be a significant variance from contracted volumes. If fewer patients are coming through than anticipated, discussions need to take place with the purchaser to understand the reasons and to address these if appropriate. If the drop in activity cannot be corrected, then the provider will probably want to negotiate to allow the funding to be spent on something else.

Some contracts do not deal with patient volumes as such. Instead, they specify when a service has to be available and to what standards it has to operate. Accident and Emergency services are contracted for in this way as are self-referral services.

PERFORMANCE MONITORING In most cases, the contract will specify what information the provider has to give the purchaser. Typically, this will consist of a monthly or quarterly report of activity against the contract specification.

The question of quality standards in NHS contracts is one of the most contentious areas of contract negotiation. Some purchasers issue quality specifications of awesome complexity requiring large amounts of information. The effort put into very detailed reporting against quality specifications can divert resources away from patient care.

Some quality standards have been imposed by the government through the Patient's Charter (Department of Health, 1991; NHSE, 1995). Box 6.3 summarizes the main requirements of the Charter.

The pursuit of high quality health care should be a shared goal between purchaser and provider and it is appropriate to develop a joint strategy on quality assurance. Such a strategy should aim to set

Box 6.3
The Patient's Charter

To receive health care on the basis of clinical need regardless of the ability to pay

Respect for privacy, dignity, religious and cultural beliefs

Ensured access to services for all including people with special needs

Clear explanation of any treatments proposed including risks and alternatives available

Immediate assessment (within five minutes) in Accident and Emergency departments

Patients to be seen within 30 minutes of appointment time in outpatient departments

Patients whose operations have been cancelled for non-medical reasons to be admitted to hospital within one month of cancellation

Guaranteed admission for treatment by a specific date no later than two years from the day included onto the waiting list

All patients to have a named nurse, midwife or health visitor responsible for planning their care

Patients to be given rights of access to their own health records

Discharge of patients should be planned prior to discharge taking into account continuing health or social care needs

Patients to be offered the choice whether or not to take part in medical research or medical student training

All complaints about any NHS services to be fully investigated and responded to in a written reply from the chief executive

Nine out of ten people can expect to be seen within 13 weeks. Everyone can expect to be seen within 26 weeks

If admitted to A and E you can expect to be given a bed within 3 hours

You have a right to be told before you go into hospital whether it is planned to care for you in a ward for men and women

achievable and worthwhile goals and to eliminate duplication of effort between purchaser and provider. A good quality assurance strategy should not involve either party in the preparation and analysis of large amounts of data.

In the longer term, there may be a move to an *accreditation system* in which providers are accredited, perhaps by an external body, as providing services of satisfactory quality. This would relieve purchasers of the onerous and expensive task of writing quality specifications and developing monitoring systems to ensure compliance. Chapter 10 discusses issues of quality in more detail.

RESOLVING Problems and disputes do arise over performance against contracts
PROBLEMS and it is important to be clear about how these will be resolved.
The key to good contract management is to make sure that a joint
problem-solving approach is taken between purchaser and provider rather than allowing matters to slip into acrimony.

The most common form of dispute tends to be about volume.
The contract anticipates a certain pattern of referrals to the
provider but neither purchaser nor provider can directly control
that flow. GPs are still free to refer to wherever they think most
appropriate for their patients and the ability to predict patient
flows for relatively small populations is still poor. It takes only a
relatively small shift in the number of emergency referrals to throw
a contract out of kilter.

In addressing this kind of problem, providers need to recognize
that purchasers do not in general have a 'slush fund' from which
they can simply pay out for additional work. Similarly, purchasers
need to recognize the ethical dilemmas which clinicians face
when there is a mismatch between the number of patients turning
up on their door-steps and the theoretical demand set out in the
contract.

The key steps in resolving disputes for both parties are:

◆ Understanding exactly what has happened.
◆ Trying to understand why it has happened.
◆ Agreeing actions to minimize damage to patients.
◆ Learning for next time.

THE ROLE OF THE It is in the interests of the provider organization, the clinician and
CLINICIAN the patient that the clinical director, in concert with the business
MANAGER IN THE manager, play a central role in the negotiation of contracts. A very
CONTRACTING basic rule for any clinician manager is:
PROCESS

> *Do not agree to a contract unless you are confident that you
> can deliver it.*

Clinical directors should lead the contracting process for their own
directorates. This does not mean that the clinical director has to be
present at each and every meeting in the contracting process. It
does mean that anyone who represents you is perfectly clear about:

◆ The fact that he or she is *representing* you.
◆ What can and cannot be agreed to on your behalf.
◆ Your objectives in contract negotiation.

It is desirable that the clinical director establishes face-to-face
contact with the people who are contracting for services. The
clinical director will have a unique perspective on the reality of the
clinical situation. He or she will be dealing with real patients and
real staff – not just sets of numbers. The clinical director should be

able to interpret the numbers and translate them into practical healthcare terms.

Preparing for contract negotiation

Negotiation is the process through which two parties starting from different positions come together to an agreed position with which they can both live.

If the starting positions are identical, no negotiation is needed. If agreement is not reached with which both parties can live, then the negotiation has failed and failed for *both* parties.

The key to successful negotiation is good preparation. Many professional negotiators use the *Like*–*Intend*–*Must* mnemonic as a framework for preparation.

Like to have

Things which you would *like* to achieve in the negotiation but which you would be prepared to concede if necessary. They are the bargaining counters of the negotiation process. Like pawns in chess, they can be sacrificed but should not simply be thrown away.

Intend to have

These are the things which you fully intend to get from your negotiation. If absolutely necessary, you may give in on some of these if the negotiation would otherwise fail.

Must have

These are the things without which the negotiation will fail anyway. Contracting for a level of activity which you can meet and securing the resources which you really need fall into this category.

What do you need to know before the negotiation

Before you start negotiating with the purchaser, negotiate with your own management colleagues. Make sure that they will give you the information you need and will do the arithmetic for you. None of it is difficult, but it is time-consuming.

You need to have some feel for the types of service which the purchaser may want to commission from you and the quantities involved. This will mean looking back over your activity figures to find out what kind of demand exists and being clear about current waiting list levels. You may also want to read the *purchasing strategy* which commissioning agencies usually produce.

You need to have proper costings for each of your services and to know how these will be affected by changes in volume. Chapter 3 addresses the questions of fixed and variable costs and their impact on prices in more detail. Ask your assigned finance officer to prepare a table of costs for each of your services for various volume assumptions. An example is given in Box 6.4.

Box 6.4
Prices for a range of
volume assumptions

Procedure	Fixed cost	Variable cost	Volume assumptions			
			50	100	150	200
Procedure 1	£10 000	£10	£210	£110	£77	£60
Procedure 2	£5000	£500	£600	£550	£533	£525

You need to think about any service developments you may wish to advocate and you need to be clear about the benefits you are claiming for these. Service developments which will result in reduced costs per case or measurable improvements in clinical outcomes will be a powerful bargaining tool. The onus is on you to demonstrate the benefits of the developments which you want to introduce.

You need to find out how competitive your prices are both locally and nationally. If your prices are out of line with other local providers, there is a good chance that you will lose the contract unless you can show that your higher price really is justified in concrete terms like readmission rates or postoperative infection rates. If you cannot show that you are better, then, quite rightly, the purchaser will buy the cheaper service. If your prices are out of line with national figures, again you are likely to come under pressure to justify your higher costs.

Try to put yourself in the purchaser's shoes. What are their *must haves, intend to haves* and *like to haves*?

Managing the negotiation   Take your business manager and assigned finance officer with you. In some cases you may also want to take a senior nurse or other specialist.

Agree with your team that they will only contribute if you ask them to. You are a negotiating *team* and you are the captain.

Set out your arguments as clearly, reasonably and persuasively as you know how. Try to agree the basics first. For how many cases of what sort should we be contracting?

Listen carefully and politely to any counter arguments. If the purchaser thinks less capacity is required than you do, ask them to explain why. Have they evidence that the incidence of a particular condition is on the decline or that GPs are recommending different treatment?

Put your prices on the table and explain them. Stress any reductions in prices which you have been able to achieve through changes in clinical practice or greater efficiency. If you have been forced to increase prices, explain why this has been unavoidable and stress the off-setting savings which have been made elsewhere.

Put forward your proposals for improving the quality of care. Stress the benefits to patients. Point out the consequences of *not* making these improvements.

Put forward your proposals for service developments and explain how these will benefit patients and benefit the purchaser.

Throughout the negotiation process:

◆ Argue persuasively.
◆ Listen attentively.
◆ Behave politely.

Be prepared to *bargain*. This might involve linking things together.

If you can agree to ... we might be able to ...

Unless the issue is very straightforward, do not agree to anything on the spot. Take it away and work it through carefully before responding. Very few contracting issues can be safely resolved on the spot with a pocket calculator.

CONCLUSION

Contracting for health will lie at the heart of the National Health Service for the foreseeable future. The contracting process will be the engine of change in the development of health care in the UK, particularly as GP fundholders come to control an increasingly large part of the purchasing function.

At the time of writing, contracting is still at a fairly primitive level. Patterns of health care have not changed radically, no major providers have 'gone out of business' and there is still very little public debate about rationing and priorities in health care.

Within the next five years, the following are likely to have happened:

◆ GPs will be the main purchasers within the NHS. As a result, the contracting dialogue will be between GPs and fellow clinicians rather than between administrators.
◆ There will be less emphasis on what we do (throughput) and much more on what we achieve (outputs).
◆ There will be some level of public debate which will make healthcare rationing decisions more explicit.
◆ Providers which are not able to demonstrate that they are delivering worthwhile health benefits at a reasonable cost will 'go out of business'.

The practical lessons for clinical directors are as follows:

◆ Make sure that you and your colleagues in other clinical disciplines are in the driving seat of contract negotiation and contract management.
◆ Make sure that you have a management team which is geared up to *support* you, not *control* you.
◆ Take the lead in developing more cost-effective models of care and make sure that you are able to demonstrate the real benefits of what you and your colleagues do.

SUMMARY

◆ The internal market in the NHS is a *managed market*. It differs in a number of important ways from the sort of *free market* in which commercial organizations operate.

◆ *Purchasers*, in the form of *health authorities, commissioning agencies* and *fundholding general practitioners* place contracts with *providers* to deliver particular healthcare services.

◆ A contract specifies the *price* which will be charged by the provider to the purchaser. The government has specified that within the NHS:

Price must always equal cost.
The same price must be charged to all NHS purchasers.

◆ One of the main areas of development in contracting is the *currency* of the contract. What are the most appropriate units for measuring health care?

◆ There is a *national timetable* for contracting. This is linked to the government's own public expenditure decisions.

◆ Contracts determine the *resources* which will be available for patient care.

◆ Contracts determine priorities in health care and often specify the *number* of patients for whom you are expected to provide care.

◆ Contracts are *negotiated* between purchasers and providers.

◆ Good *preparation* is the key to successful negotiation.

◆ Contracts are of such fundamental importance to the success of your unit and your ability to provide good patient care that clinical directors have to *lead* the contract negotiation process.

CONTRACTING CHECKLIST

◆ Do you clearly lead the contract negotiations for your directorate?

◆ Do you have accurate and well-presented information about the demands on your service and the levels of work which you have done?

◆ Do you have accurate financial information which enables you to see the true costs of each type of care which you provide?

◆ Do you have accurate financial information which lets you see the effects on costs of different volumes of activity?

◆ Do you have a support team to help you in preparing for and conducting contract negotiations?

◆ Do you have accurate and timely information which enables you to monitor the performance of your directorate against its contracts?

♦ Do your clinical colleagues accept the need to work within a contractual framework?

♦ Have you a process in place to assess the value of the work, which you do so that it can be clearly demonstrated?

♦ Do you have a rolling programme of 'product development' which enables you to develop and implement models of care which are demonstrably more cost-effective?

♦ Do you have a strategy for moving towards providing complete packages of care?

FURTHER READING

♦ Koch, H. (1991), *Total Quality Management in Health-care*, Longman Press, London.

♦ Koch, H. (1992), *Implementing and sustaining Total Quality*, Longman Press, London.

Although these two books are expensive, they provide valuable information on a wide range of quality topics and are useful tools for dipping into to find examples and guidance for developing quality initiatives.

♦ Department of Health (1991), *The Patient's Charter – Raising the Standard*, London.

This booklet provides full details of the rights and standards set out in the Patient's Charter.

Contracting

♦ NHSME (1989), *Contracting for Health Services.*

Quite detailed direction on how contracts should be developed and used.

REFERENCES

Department of Health (1991), *The Patient's Charter – Raising the Standard.* London.

Manning, S. and Dunning, M. (1994), Every day in every way. *Health Service Journal*, 10 March, 27–29.

NHSE (1995), *Revised and Expanded Patient's Charter: Implementation.* HSG (95) 13.

Raftery, J. and Gibson, G. (1994), Banking on knowledge. *Health Service Journal*, 10 February, 28–30.

DEVELOPING CLINICAL SERVICES

Kingsley Manning

OBJECTIVES

♦ To identify the forces driving the changes in the provision of clinical services and the opportunities this offers.

♦ To show how competitor advantage can be achieved through market analysis and the development of the appropriate business case.

♦ To examine the components of competitive advantage.

♦ To show how to develop a business case in the context of a Trust's strategic development.

INTRODUCTION

For nearly four decades the steady state structure of the NHS gave the UK health industry a remarkable and often misleading sense of stability. The illusion of rational planning provided a sense of security whereby sensible men agreed between them what was required and the system was persuaded to deliver it. In practice what the system delivered was haphazard and sometimes wasteful, delivering new hospitals where they were not needed and often duplicating services. Clinical services within a particular hospital were often developed in response to a specific consultant's enthusiasm or parachuted in by some decision at regional or national level.

Whatever the weaknesses of the approach, from the clinicians' point of view it did have advantages. Clinicians could often get the developments they sought without getting embroiled in the consequent administrative and managerial burden. The protective veil around clinicians has now gone for ever, torn away not only by the government's reforms but by the underlying forces which prompted them. If clinicians are to continue to provide leadership in the development of clinical services they need now to acquire new skills about determining needs, justifying costs and selling benefits.

Against this rapidly evolving background the opportunities for developing new services will abound, coming from changes in technology, particularly information technology, in combination with changes in the industrial structure. The skill that clinicians will increasingly need will be the ability to spot where developments in both converge. This will require constant monitoring and the gathering of intelligence about the developing marketplace; for clinicians, academic journals and research conferences will no longer be enough. Below are described some of the major changes which clinicians may wish to review periodically in the context of their own service and which will give rise to challenging new opportunities.

TECHNOLOGY DRIVEN CHANGE

For the last three or four decades the shape of clinical services and, therefore, the opportunities for development have been driven largely by changes in clinical technology. Pharmaceutical developments, endoscopy and changes in anaesthetics are all examples of developments that have resulted in major changes in clinical practice and service strategy. In the future, however, the major changes will be driven not so much by changes in clinical technology but by the all pervasive effect of information technology. To a remarkable extent, healthcare services in the UK have been unaffected by the revolution that has changed other service industries so dramatically. As a result much of health care remains resolutely low technology, based on the personal interaction between the carer or clinician and the patient.

There are three major trends in technology affecting the development of clinical services. First, major developments and significant breakthroughs are likely to occur with declining frequency as the scale, cost and length of the required research programmes increase inexorably. Threshold costs of new technologies are therefore going to continue to rise, driven upwards by this increasing complexity and rising regulatory requirements. The increasing costs, complexity and integration requirements of these new technologies will tend to focus development and introduction on a declining number of centres.

Second, as the costs of new technology rise, existing technology will become cheaper and more widely distributed. The constantly falling prices of the fundamental components of computing power will ensure that many diagnostic and treatment technologies will become much cheaper, easier to use and more reliable. This will not only allow such technologies to be widely distributed but also fundamentally change the human skill base.

These two trends also hold true for the pharmaceutical industry. The introduction of major new drugs is becoming rarer and very much more expensive. At the same time many existing drug therapies are reaching the end of their patent lives, at which time prices will tend to fall. As a result, after years of focusing almost exclusively on the research and development of new chemistry, pharmaceutical companies are becoming very interested in integrated drug delivery mechanisms and services.

Finally, the major and most important developments in clinical services will be driven by information technology. The declining costs of computer processing will enable powerful information management tools to be applied to healthcare services changing the way in which those services are delivered. The analysis and availability in 'real time' of patient and operational information will lead to an increasingly multi-skilled workforce, with rising levels of productivity, offering patients sophisticated packages of care. In North America, information technology is at present the largest single investment area for the healthcare industry – an industry which is now probably the largest customer for the major computer companies and where they are focusing an increasing proportion of their development effort.

THE SHIFTING INDUSTRIAL STRUCTURE

Shifts in technology combined with the evolving framework of the NHS are bringing about a radical change in the structure of the UK health industry. Such changes in any industry give rise both to threats to existing services as well as providing new opportunities. The long-term stability of the NHS has meant that now change is occurring, it is ever more complicated and rapid.

Underpinning the shifts in industrial structure are the changing patterns of need and demand. By comparison to most industries, and within limits, healthcare needs and demands are highly predictable and the reducing cost of computing power will increasingly make accurate information about both needs readily available. In health care, complications arise because of different judgements as to what is legitimate need and actual demand. As a result, many of the generalizations made about demand rapidly do not stand up when applied to particular locations and services. Box 7.1 gives some examples.

Thus the analysis required to support the development of expanded or new clinical services must be based on the appropriate and service-specific population. Such an analysis will, however, only show the predicted need and potential demand. In practice the actual demand is determined increasingly by the purchasing decisions of the health authorities and GP fundholders.

In terms of the development of clinical services, the key impact of the government's NHS reforms has been to clarify responsibility. Clinicians and their provider units can propose but GP fundholders and health authorities make the decisions. Both of these groups are cash limited and both will have their own and often different priorities. Although the overall NHS budget continues to grow, in real terms much of the growth is eaten up by increasing demands

Box 7.1

◆ There is a general growth in the over 60 population: this is by no means universal, for the UK as a whole the over 65s will grow by 8% over the next 10 years, but in one North London borough the same population will actually decline by 28%, and indeed it is very uncertain what pattern of need today's 50 year old will exhibit in ten years time.

◆ Whilst the overall demand for health care is generally thought to be rising, specific demand for particular services, such as Accident and Emergency attendances, is stable and in some areas, actually declining.

◆ In health care the supply of a service will tend to generate demand. There is considerable evidence that the provision of more elderly care beds encourages higher usage, with admission thresholds nearly always adjusting to achieve 100% occupancy.

built into the current pattern of provision. For most purchasers new or expanded clinical services can only be funded by diverting spending from elsewhere. This underlines the reality that prioritization – rationing for large groups of the population, is now the responsibility of the purchasers; explicitly for health authorities and implicitly for GP fundholders.

The priorities of both these groups will often differ from provider based clinicians. The performance of purchasers is measured crudely in terms of rising levels of activity which requires reducing unit costs, whilst at the same time improving general levels of health status. Health authorities are therefore primarily concerned with the health of their total population and are increasingly looking for clinical services which maximize their leverage, that is have the greatest impact on the local health status relevant to spend. GP fundholders are naturally more parochial in their interests, concerned with buying on a short-term cycle convenient, high quality services for their own patients.

These purchasers are, however, combining to shift the focus of service delivery away from traditional hospital services. Technological development permits, financial constraints require and consumers demand that a greater proportion of services are delivered in more cost-effective formats closer to the patient, in and around their own home.

Both groups are also becoming much more interested in demonstrable, measurable outcome benefits. Very rapidly over the next few years all clinical services, not just new ones, will be expected to provide purchasers with data about their outcomes. Some clinicians may well feel threatened by this development, but increasingly sophisticated purchasers, supported by consumer interest and legal imperatives, will not be diverted from demanding what benefit is likely to come from a treatment and how well it is being performed.

This shift of purchasing power within the NHS is occurring at the same time as an increasing over capacity of traditional service provision. This over capacity is being driven by new clinical and service technology, in combination with only modest growth in the demand for services. Even though large tranches of capacity have been taken out of the NHS the potential capacity of what remains, still exceeds substantially the ability of the system to pay for its use. The maintenance of waiting lists for some areas of treatment, represent a lack of purchasing capacity not of provider capacity. Indeed, the total existing waiting list amounts to less then eight weeks output of the current providers.

This structural over-capacity is further exacerbated by reductions in entry barriers for new providers whilst the exit barriers for current providers remain very high. Whilst the reducing costs of existing technology are increasingly allowing local hospitals to enter the traditional high technology preserves of the big city hospitals, it remains politically very difficult to close hospitals. This reduction in entry barriers, whilst benefiting many providers, allowing them to contemplate developing new services that even a few years ago would have been out of the question, also raises the level of competitiveness within the industry. If one hospital can consider introducing a new service, then its neighbour down the road is probably equally capable of developing the same service. Furthermore, given the relative rigidity of hospital costs, current providers of the service are unlikely to voluntarily give up in the face of a new competitor.

Even given improving information about outcomes and service quality, purchasing decisions will remain infuriatingly idiosyncratic in the eyes of many clinicians. Purchasers, in the absence of overwhelming evidence of benefits, are likely to remain with the current providers.

ACHIEVING COMPETITIVE ADVANTAGE

The changing structure of the healthcare industry will make it both more difficult and more important for those developing new clinical services to establish some distinct competitive advantage. Fragmented, better informed purchasing combined with lower entry barriers and over capacity, will ensure that past referral patterns, often based on historic ties and customs, will come under increasing pressure. Furthermore, given the generic nature of much of health care, both in terms of treatments and patient needs, the opportunities for achieving competitive advantage are limited.

In any industry competitive advantage stems from one of two positions:

◆ *Price advantage* where a supplier through superior asset and labour productivity is the lowest cost provider within the defined marketplace, or

◆ *Differentiation* where a supplier offers a distinct service or product, with few directly similar offerings from other suppliers.

Price advantage is mostly clearly linked with volume. In health care, as in most other industries the learning curve effect and economies of scale both apply. The higher volume of a particular treatment performed the more expertise acquired and the greater the opportunity to increase productivity, coupled with the ability to spread fixed costs and overheads over a greater number of cases. Typically in health care, volume is limited by access and therefore by local population densities. Smaller providers will therefore be able to sustain higher prices for generic procedures where they are isolated from centres of population. In effect, for many straightforward procedures relative prices are a function of ease of access for patients.

However, patients, encouraged by their purchasers and enabled by growing affluence, are becoming more mobile and more discerning. Therefore in the absence of underlying volume in demand, developing a service on the basis that it is going to be cheaper than the hospital down the road is very risky. In most cases this strategy will only be successful if the resulting cost/price differentiation is very significant – perhaps in the order of 10 or 20%. To achieve this will require the new service to be fundamentally different from that currently on offer. This can perhaps be achieved by investing in a significant piece of new technology, or radically altering current working practices in ways that other providers would find difficult to replicate. Given that 60 to 70% of costs are labour costs, improvements in labour productivity are the crucial area where a significant advantage can be gained.

Labour pay rates remain, however, very similar across all UK healthcare providers and changes in clinical technology flow from one provider to another very rapidly; as a result minor differences in costs, given rising purchaser awareness, will be ironed out of the system fairly quickly. Introducing a new clinical service simply on the basis of a minor price advantage is very unlikely to be successful. Given the high exit barriers for most providers discussed above, this is likely to result in a damaging increase in overall capacity for all concerned.

Competitive advantage through differentiation can be achieved in a number of ways, but it all depends on those making the buying decisions seeing and appreciating the difference. If the buyers do not value those distinctive elements then it will leave their decision unaffected, particularly if they are being asked to pay a higher price for the differentiated service. In health care the primary sources of differentiation are:

♦ Quality.
♦ Technology.
♦ Service content.
♦ Brand.

The concept of *quality* has been greatly debased in health care because of a widespread collusion that all NHS services are of the highest possible quality – the notion that some providers' services are of positively better quality than their neighbours, being politically unacceptable. The UK has an astonishing number of hospitals who claim to be international centres of excellence. Thankfully this situation is changing, as both purchasers with clinical expertise and patients are becoming more demanding.

Healthcare quality has two overlapping aspects: service quality, how the patient perceives they are dealt with, the standard of accommodation and so forth; and clinical quality, whether or not the diagnosis and treatment was performed properly and had a positive outcome. In both cases the key issues concern expectations, perceptions and measurement. In terms of service quality, expectations are rising on the tide of consumerism. In terms of clinical quality the dam is about to burst. Purchasers, soon to be followed by patients, have rising expectations that clinical quality will be measured and that information will be freely available.

The chief difficulty for strategies based on differentiation through quality is with purchaser and patient perceptions. Patients are most likely to be persuaded by tangible evidence of service quality whilst purchasers are probably more concerned with clinical quality. In both cases the quality concerns and priorities of the clinicians delivering the service may not be shared or appreciated by those using them or paying for them. In all cases it is, therefore, important when developing any new clinical services that quality standards are made explicit, are prestated and are measurable.

Technological differentiation in health care has been widespread, with the acquisition of a key piece of equipment or skilled individual or team marking out a provider. Such differentiation remains very possible particularly if opportunities are exploited around information technology as discussed above. However, it may have been possible to sustain such a strategy for a significant period; increasingly, the short diffusion times and lower costs of technology may mean that a technological lead is eroded in a matter of a few years. To work, this approach must therefore be based on a continual renewal of the technological advantage through reinvestment and training. Technological differentiation is now a function of this ability to keep at the forefront of developments rather the simple periodic acquisition of an exciting piece of new equipment. Investing in the latest equipment will provide only a temporary advantage if it is not coupled with a continuing development programme, placing an increasing premium on clinical and research skills and their application to patient treatment.

Service content is an important form of differentiation for common or generic services. It is difficult to persuade most people that one cataract treatment is different from another but if diagnosis and treatment are integrated into a single day, with waiting times guaranteed to be less than 10 days, then a common treatment becomes special for both purchasers and patients. The key to such strategies tends to lie with the integration of a number of different service elements, which are normally provided separately, perhaps using the binding power of information technology. The development of integrated service packages for common areas of treatment can produce a very distinct service with considerable appeal and the prospect of identifiable, manageable and reducible costs.

Brands are always important in markets with complex products and services, no more so than in health care. Where the content and benefits of a service are difficult to understand and compare then consumers will put great faith in the provider's track record and name. The major teaching hospitals have always exploited the feeling of security they provide to patients, which often outweighs poor service and sometimes mediocre clinical quality. Even in a local community, brands are very important. The reputation of a local hospital, service or even individual clinician is a tender asset which needs active cultivation. In practice, however, there are limitations as to the application of brand to new developments. Creating a brand takes time and therefore is usually not possible. Exploiting an existing brand is very possible but usually only works if there is consistency with the brand's original values. If a hospital has a famous reputation for a particular service it may not be transferable to an unrelated service. It must also be remembered that a brand is only sustainable if the service delivered consistently fulfils the brand's promise. If a provider takes its brand position for granted then its value can be rapidly eroded.

Successful differentiation strategies will combine effectively a number of different elements, for example, technological skills with a major brand name or service content with service quality. In most cases the more elements of differentiation for a service the stronger the competitive advantage.

In some cases successful differentiation can sustain a price premium, with purchasers prepared to pay more for a better service. Maintaining a differentiated service may, however, also cost more, requiring perhaps higher spending on technology or better qualified staff. The price premiums that can be achieved are unlikely to be substantial, particularly in health care. Therefore high productivity – squeezing the cost base as much as possible – is just as important for a differentiated strategy as for a price strategy.

COMPETITOR ANALYSIS

A key step in formulating the strategy for a new clinical service must be to analyse the current or potential advantage of competitors. The sources of advantage available to other providers are of course the same, based on price or differentiation. There is always a danger of failing to appreciate a competitor's strengths and it is, therefore, very important to rely primarily on the views of those who make the purchasing decisions or who use the service. Although their decisions may be 'misguided' they are also always going to be 'right'.

Simply replicating a competitor's strengths is unlikely to prove successful. Purchasers are unlikely to spot the difference and are therefore likely to stay with the service they know. More appealing will be a strategy which offers a contrast to existing services effectively highlighting weaknesses in the competitor's position.

Wherever consumers have a choice, providers have to create some competitive advantage if they wish to survive. In the UK healthcare consumer choice is broadening and becoming more evident. At the same time the range of potential providers of service is increasing. Therefore any consideration of a new clinical development must include an explicit analysis of how any competitive advantage is going to be achieved and sustained. If those proposing the new development cannot argue convincingly that the new service has some clear attraction and advantages over existing services then why should any patient use it or purchaser pay for it?

THE SERVICE PORTFOLIO

Very few clinical services exist in isolation in any hospital or community unit. Most are part of a portfolio of services which needs to have its own coherence and logic. At the simplest level services will use common support functions and the greater the common use, the lower the cost and greater the possibility of higher support service quality. The most attractive new clinical services are those that exploit or extend existing support service assets or skills. Similarly, with skills and technology, step changes for organizations, taking them into fields where they have little previous experience are always the most difficult to bring off. Building on existing strengths is always much easier and less risky.

Portfolio consistency also applies strategically. It is very difficult for an organization which has traditionally competed on low price to introduce a new premium priced high technology service. Similarly a well known brand name associated with cardiac surgery will not be transferable to plastic surgery. Such strategies are difficult for organizations to implement successfully because they may require different management skills and because they often lack credibility with purchasers and consumers.

Most Trusts are forced to ration the number of new developments that they can take forward at any one time; not only because of the lack of a bottomless pit of investment funds but more importantly because of limited managerial resources – it is better to do a few things successfully. Therefore, clinicians proposing new developments are likely to be faced with competition from other colleagues for the Trust's selected support. Projects which extend, complement and therefore strengthen the existing service portfolio are likely to be much more appealing than those that take the Trust into new and possibly uncertain territory.

THE BUSINESS CASE   The management of the service portfolio is a key element of a Trust's annual production of a strategic direction and business case, documents which together set out the development path of the organization over the coming years, including the introduction of new services. The Trust is likely to have a number of opportunities and, therefore, to help consider which to take forward and to test the robustness of each, it is likely to ask for a business case to be prepared to support potential development.

For clinicians the ability to lead in the preparation of a convincing business case is a crucial skill. However obvious the various benefits of a new development, it will not gain support unless they can be expressed in terms which are both clinically and managerially attractive. The business case must demonstrate how the new clinical development delivers measurable, tangible benefits to patients, to the Trust and ultimately to the purchasers.

The key purpose of a business case is to assemble, in a single document, the relevant information about a project to allow all concerned to make a judgement about its desirability and viability. The first audience for the case is its authors; it provides an opportunity for those promoting the development to test their assumptions and check its feasibility. The second audience will be the management of the host provider organization, anxious to support developments contributing to the organization's growth and prosperity but always concerned to avoid risks given its limited resources for investment. The final audience will be the purchasers who will often have to underwrite the developments if it is to proceed and who have competing calls on their support.

The business case must therefore address different audiences, with clarity and directness at a premium. Whilst the business case must 'sell' the development, this is most likely to be achieved if it provides a balanced appraisal of both the opportunity and associated risks. A business case is not, however, a scientific paper. Often the underlying data will be weak or incomplete, projections of costs revenues and timescale uncertain. The quality of a business case comes not from the spurious and superficial accuracy of page upon page of financial projections but from an obvious coherence and integrity. A business case is ultimately about probability; about the likelihood of achieving predicted outcomes and revenues within the planned timescale. It is therefore about presenting the evidence and assessing risk, often using incomplete information. A key element of this process is therefore the consideration of a range of options. The clinicians concerned will normally have a clearly preferred plan, but the best way of testing this is to consider how else and by whom the same service objectives could be achieved.

There is a great danger, however, of the business case process becoming too important and a temptation to make the consideration of a new clinical development an exercise in business planning rather than a creative analysis of the critical issues.

The business case must assimilate the points outlined in Box 7.2 into one cogently argued document.

Box 7.2
The business case

♦ The objectives of the new service.

♦ The options available to the Trust which may include other ways of achieving the objectives, perhaps by a more gradual approach.

♦ The comparative costs and benefits associated with each of the options, including both financial and non-financial information.

♦ The reasons for selecting the preferred option along with the detailed capital expenditure implications. This should include an assessment of the material risks associated with the preferred option, their quantification where possible through sensitivity analysis and a description of the infrastructure to be established to manage these risks.

♦ The assumptions underlying the market for the services to be delivered by the investment. The robustness of these assumptions will be critically important where the success of the new investment is predicated upon either higher costs or higher volumes. In such cases the involvement of purchasers and their commitment to the underlying assumptions will be a prerequisite for approval.

In considering the business case, the Trust Board will need to check, within the overall framework of the Trust's development, that the proposed new clinical service:

♦ Offers real value for money.

♦ Has not overlooked options that should sensibly have been considered.

♦ Will be more cost effective than the alternatives.

♦ Will deliver the promised benefits.

In particular, the Trust Board will need to be sure that the business case is compatible with its purchasers' plans and that the business case fairly reflects the understanding and commitment of the relevant purchasers.

Not surprisingly there are copious guidelines available from the NHS Executive as to how to produce a business case. This guidance is primarily for Trusts seeking approval for capital investments. Irrespective of any need for capital investment, it is likely that a Trust Board will wish all business cases presented to use a structure compatible with that required by the NHS Executive. A proposed structure and content, derived from the NHS Guidelines, is set out in Box 7.3, and involves seven steps.

Box 7.3
NHS proposed
structure and content
for a business case

1. Strategic context.

2. Objectives and benefit criteria.

3. Options.

4. Benefits.

5. Associated costs.

6. Sensitivity to risk.

7. Preferred option.

1. Establishing the strategic context

The most important requirement for any new service development is that it forms part of a well defined service strategy. Service strategies are formulated and documented on an annual basis in each NHS Trust's Strategic Direction. The strategic context of a new development should be placed within the framework established by the Trust's Strategic Direction.

Understanding the local market within which an NHS Trust operates is essential for ascertaining the need for the new service. Such an understanding will require knowledge of the present and future purchasing intentions of local health authorities and GP fundholders as well as the likely developments in provision of comparable services by local NHS and private sector competitors. The support of a range of purchasers should, where possible, be secured at the outset. This is best achieved by clinicians and clinical directors meeting purchasers directly in the company of the appropriate trust managers.

In assessing future levels of demand and supply, it will be necessary to take full account of the pressures for change to current patterns of service delivery. Such pressures include:

◆ Sub-Regional and Regional reviews.
◆ Changes in capitation funding.
◆ NHS policy initiatives such as community care.
◆ Demographic, social and technological changes.

The existing service profile and purchasers' intentions provide the best indicators of existing and developing market demand. The service facilities needed to satisfy this demand will determine the need for change to the existing configuration of local healthcare resources. All business case proposals for new developments should be driven by a service strategy which aims to meet identified needs for health care and health gain. However, the affordability of new service solutions is a critical constraint on the business case.

2. Define objectives and benefit criteria

The objectives of the service development must be set so that they will contribute to the general objectives of the NHS Trust set out in its Strategic Direction and annual business case. The objectives should be sufficiently detailed so that the broad service aims are clear but should also be formulated so as to invite a number of options.

Benefit criteria are used to evaluate and ultimately select the options available for achieving the service objectives. Benefit criteria fall into three categories:

◆ Benefits which can be quantified financially.
◆ Benefits which can be quantified but not in financial terms, such as improved clinical outcomes.
◆ Benefits which cannot easily be quantified, such as enhanced service quality.

3. Generate options

The purpose of this process is to identify as wide a range of options as possible, available to meet the service objectives. From a comprehensive review, a shortlist of the most feasible options will be compiled which will then be subject to formal cost benefit analysis. The 'Do nothing' or 'Do minimum' option should be retained as a baseline in the shortlist.

4. Measure benefits

The benefits of the short-listed options will be measured using the benefit criteria established earlier. Where possible, all benefits should be quantified. Constructing weighted benefit scores is preferable to simple ranking of options and the weighting process should invite participation from a wide cross-section of interested parties.

5. Identify and quantify associated costs

The net costs of the short-listed options will need to be identified and quantified in order to complete the cost benefit analysis. This will require an estimate of:

♦ Capital costs.
♦ Revenue costs.
♦ Opportunity costs of resources already being used which will be displaced.
♦ Any capital or revenue costs that would be borne by others outside the Trust.

The period of appraisal should normally equate to the intended period of use of any underlying capital asset. As well as the quantity of costs, the timing of these costs should be identified and discounted to a net present cost using a 6% real discount rate.

Once the evaluation has identified the total and discounted cash costs of all short-listed options the affordability of each will need to be tested with purchasers. In general, investments which increase the total revenue costs of the NHS Trust without increasing the volume of activity that can be absorbed will be difficult to justify.

6. Assess sensitivity to risk

Earlier stages of the appraisal process will have been completed on the basis of assumptions made concerning uncertain future circumstances such as purchasing capacity, construction costs, revenue costs, manpower savings or timing of costs. Sensitivity analysis is a process by which the impact on the investment proposal of changes in the basis of assumptions made is measured. The most robust options are those which, even if the assumptions upon which they are based turn out to be different, deliver the same benefits with only marginal changes in costs. The aim of sensitivity analysis is to identify options which minimize the major risks.

7. Identify the preferred option

The conclusion of the outline business case comes with the identification of the preferred option. This step should state the key factors which make the preferred option superior to the other short-listed options.

Risk management strategy Risk and uncertainty are inherent in any new development. The business case must, therefore, demonstrate how risks are to be managed and minimized and, in addition, what action will be taken should problems arise. The risk management strategy will draw on the findings of the sensitivity analysis in identifying the material risks and will then go on to identify counter measures which will be implemented either to pre-empt the risk or, should the risk crystallize, to minimize its effect. Measures may include, for example, negotiating flexible contractual agreements with contractors or providing for delay in the project timescales.

IMPLEMENTATION In all organizations there is a danger of new developments failing not at the business case stage but in their implementation. There is a natural temptation for those directly concerned to relax their interest once approval for a new project has been won. In practice the work has only but just begun. The successful implementation of the new development is critically dependent on the management and leadership from the associated clinicians.

Project A detailed discussion of clinical service project management is
management given in Chapter 8. In the context of developing clinical services, effective project management is a primary requirement for success. The availability of good project management skills, even if these have to be 'bought-in', should be considered in preparing the business case. Indeed if sufficient, good implementation skills are not available then the risks of pursuing the development may overwhelm the potential benefits. The diversionary effect on existing services of a poorly implemented new development can be ruinous.

Marketing and A key component of that implementation has to be the marketing
selling and selling. As discussed above, the competitive climate for clinical services is confused. Even the most attractive and sound new development will not necessarily command the appropriate attention of potential purchasers.

Clinicians have the central and key role in this process. However professional and enthusiastic the marketing support provided by the unit, this cannot substitute for the clinicians directly involved. Patient referrals lie in the hands of other clinicians, usually GPs, who are mostly persuaded of the benefits of a new development by other doctors rather than a ubiquitous business manager. Similarly, purchasers are most susceptible to the reasoned presentation of a clinical professional. But the selling process must not be limited to doctors but extended to all members of the team, not least the nurses.

A full marketing and selling programme must form an integral part of the original business case and be available for implementation once approval for the new development has been given. The key elements of that programme are listed in Box 7.4.

Box 7.4
Key elements of a
marketing and selling
programme

◆ *Identification* of all the target purchasers and buyers, knowing who you are trying to sell to is the first step.

◆ *Communications* with all the relevant groups and individuals, briefing them about the development ahead of its launch and ensuring that they appreciate its potential benefits.

◆ *Contacting* the key purchasers and buyers in a systematic and personal fashion several times during the months before and after the launch of the new development.

◆ *Following up* early users of the new service to check satisfaction and reinforce in their minds the benefits as well as identifying areas where further improvements could be made.

CONCLUSION   Some clinicians have difficulty with the notion of marketing and selling, though in practice successful clinicians have always been effective, if sometimes eccentric, salesmen of their own ideas and talents. If a clinician wants to develop a new service then having to sell its services would seem a small price to pay.

SUMMARY

◆ Continued change is endemic in health care prompted by technological developments and changing consumer expectations.

◆ Continuing change provides the opportunity for developing new clinical services but only if they can meet existing need and demand more cost effectively.

◆ All new services must establish a distinct, defensible competitive advantage.

◆ New developments need to be the subject of a business case which tests the robustness of its clinical and economic viability.

◆ Successful developments depend more than anything else on effective implementation, led by clinicians.

FURTHER READING

♦ British Association of Medical Managers, British Medical Association, Institute of Health Services Management, Royal College of Nursing (1993), *Managing Clinical Services: a Consensus Statement of Principles for Effective Clinical Management*, Institute of Health Service Management, London.

♦ *The Clinician in Management*, the journal of *The British Association of Medical Managers*, published by Churchill Livingstone.

♦ Cowling, A. and Newman, K. Turning Doctors into Managers: An evaluation of a major NHS initiative to improve the managerial capabilities of medical consultants. *Human Resource Management Journal*, 4(4).

♦ Dawson *et al.* (1995) Management, competition and professional practice: medicine and the market place. *British Journal of Management*, forthcoming.

♦ Pettigrew *et al.* (1992), *Shaping Strategic Change*, Sage Publications, London.

♦ White, A. (1993), *Management for Clinicians*, Edward Arnold, London.

CHAPTER 8

PROJECT MANAGEMENT

David Savage

David Savage

OBJECTIVES

- ◆ To provide a step-by-step guide to establishing and running a project.

- ◆ To show how to evaluate the progress of a project.

- ◆ To examine the specific management issues raised by construction, information technology and organizational change projects.

INTRODUCTION

This chapter will cover: the different stages of a project, emphasizing those aspects where both clinical input and managerial control are essential, some common project management methodologies and finally specific issues in managing construction, information technology and organizational projects.

Box 8.1 lists some key questions that clinicians should focus their limited time on to ensure that their objectives are met:

Box 8.1
Key questions in
project management

- ◆ Is this the right project?

- ◆ Do the compromises made to secure resources (money, buildings, land) make the final outcome unacceptable?

- ◆ How do I know if a project is being well organized?

- ◆ What are the key things to monitor to ensure that a project is on track?

What is a project?

A project can be loosely defined as anything that is not part of the regular activity of the hospital. It should have a beginning and an end, with defined objectives focusing exclusively on the implementation of change. A project requires specific resourcing, usually from capital rather than revenue funding. It can include stopping something, for example closing a hospital, as well as starting something new. Projects may cover some or all of the following:

♦ Provision of new facilities or equipment.
♦ Alteration or introduction of information systems.
♦ Significant development or transfer of services.
♦ Changes to organizations or staff.

A project has five stages:

♦ Identification, specification, selection and resourcing.
♦ Planning.
♦ Execution.
♦ Completion.
♦ Evaluation.

IDENTIFICATION, SELECTION AND RESOURCING OR 'HOW TO GET YOUR HANDS ON THE MONEY'

This is often the most frustrating and difficult part of any project due to the chronic shortage of capital and the bureaucratic nature of the NHS. We will first look at general principles that can be applied to any potential project and then examine procedures and requirements specific to the NHS.

A project will often start as an individual's bright idea and different parties may have very fixed notions of the desired outcome. However, it is important to adopt a rigorous and logical approach to ensure that the intuitive ideas or preconceptions are correct and that no other solutions are available (Figure 8.1). The formality and time spent will depend on the size, complexity and likely conflict of interest of the parties involved.

Defining objectives

Objectives should be sufficiently detailed so that the broad service aims are clear, but not so specific that they preclude consideration

Figure 8.1
Option appraisal process

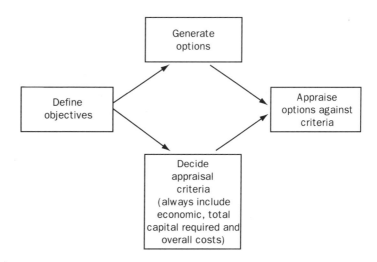

of a range of options. The objectives or goals need to be clear, so that we know when we have arrived. Objectives should be defined in terms of the benefits sought (Box 8.2). They will need to be congruent with the wider strategic vision of the hospital.

Box 8.2
Defining objectives

> Objectives may be described in terms of:
>
> ♦ Quality, e.g. reducing postoperative wound infection by 25%.
>
> ♦ Service, e.g. diagnosing and initiating therapy in all cardiac referrals from general practitioners within six weeks.
>
> ♦ Cost, e.g. reducing the cost per case for cardiac catheterization by 30%.
>
> ♦ Time, e.g. having a new facility operational before closing the old site.
>
> ♦ Scope, e.g. serving a population of a million.
>
> ♦ Meeting statutory or regulatory requirements which would inhibit or prevent an existing service from being maintained.

Alternative options   Once the objectives have been defined the next stage is to generate alternative options to meet these objectives. The options should initially cover as wide a scope as possible:

♦ The consequences of making no changes, commonly called the 'do nothing' option.
♦ A range of capital expenditures.
♦ Alternative sites and configurations for projects requiring new or altered buildings.
♦ Alternative means of service delivery, e.g. instead of building a new pathology laboratory the service could be provided by another hospital or by a private laboratory. This has been termed 'outsourcing' or 'market testing'.

A brainstorming session with the key people involved is often a good way of generating options at the outset. Early clinical input, from the ultimate users, is important to ensure that potential changes in clinical practice, patient quality and service are considered and understood. This initial list of options needs to be reduced to a manageable number (between three and six) by considering the following:

♦ How might a sceptical bank manager consider the options? Thus a minimum capital outlay option and the 'do nothing' option should be included.

♦ Are the options representative of the full range of potential feasible solutions to achieve the objectives?

♦ Do the options meet some criteria fully and most criteria partially?

Economic criteria   Economic criteria must always be considered in project appraisal. One appraisal criterion in the NHS is always total capital costs because of the chronic shortage of capital available from the Treasury. This may become less important as private sector finance becomes available.

Revenue costs are also extremely important. Revenue costs are the annual running costs which include financing costs. Financing costs are a combination of interest costs on the capital and depreciation to enable the assets to be replaced in the future.

There are several ways of combining capital and revenue costs to give a single economic measure. Two of the most common are net present value and 'payback period'.

Net present value (NPV) involves two stages: firstly, calculating the actual cash flows (capital outlays being treated as negative, revenue savings as positive) in each year of the project; secondly, discounting cash flows in future years by a fixed percentage every year (how this percentage is determined is complex, but for most NHS, publicly funded projects 6% is commonly used) to account for the fact that a pound today is worth more and a pound in a year's time (even if you did not need it today you could invest it in a savings account and earn interest making it worth more in a year's time); and summing to give the NPV. The higher the NPV, the more attractive the project.

'Payback period' is the number of years required to repay the initial capital outlay from the revenue savings made as a result of the initial investment without discounting future cash flows. It has the advantage of being simple to calculate and understand although it is not as accurate as NPV.

Assigning monetary values to project elements   Some elements of projects can be costed relatively accurately, e.g. equipment. Other areas are more problematic and may need extensive analysis, e.g. the staff savings generated by combining two sites into one or by installing a computer system. The amount of time and effort devoted to refining the economic impact of different elements will depend on:

♦ How much it influences the selection decision.
♦ Its value both absolute and relative.
♦ The increase in predictive accuracy achievable.

Non-economic criteria   To the extent that not all benefits can be quantified economically, it is necessary to identify and assess these against the options. Examples of non-economic criteria include:

♦ Better access for disabled patients.
♦ Staff and patient satisfaction.

Other criteria which may benefit the whole community, but not necessarily the hospital or even the purchasing agencies, may also need to be considered; for example:

♦ Prevention and screening programmes which may extend people's working and overall life expectancy.
♦ Minimally invasive therapies which may be more costly but enable patients to return to work more quickly.

The options can then be assessed and the preferred option selected by:

♦ Ranking the options against the economic and non-economic criteria collectively, *or*
♦ Ranking the options against the criteria individually, *or*
♦ Weighting the criteria, ranking the options against the criteria individually and producing a composite weighted benefit score.

This should be undertaken by the key stakeholders in the project, sometimes including purchasers.

Risk and sensitivity analysis

In any project assessment we are trying to predict the future – for example the costs of buildings, equipment or staff. As with any prediction of the future there is a degree of uncertainty. The purpose of risk and sensitivity analysis is to examine the assumptions on which the assessment is made and test the sensitivity of the outcome (e.g. NPV) to changes in the assumptions either individually or collectively. Examples of key assumptions might include market demand, pricing, staffing levels or utilization rates. Those assumptions that particularly affect the outcome may need to be reviewed in more depth to reduce risk. For example, if market demand and pricing are critical then commitments from customers might be required in advance to guarantee income. This is common in areas such as electricity production where contracts are often signed with customers prior to building the power station.

There is a developing trend towards the use of private capital in the NHS, whether leasing an item of equipment (for example, a CT scanner) or entire projects. Private capital requires a greater certainty that there will be a return on investment and the financiers will insist on a rigorous risk and sensitivity analysis to quantify and minimize the chances of default.

Approving projects in the NHS

The level of rigour in appraising projects in the NHS is determined by the amount of capital required:

♦ More than £10 million requires Treasury approval.
♦ More than £1 million requires approval from the NHS Management Executive.

◆ Less than £1 million is usually decided internally by Trusts within their annual capital allocation, known as the external financing limit (EFL).

◆ For any public sector procurement over 125 000 ECUs (about £100 000) a formal procedure including advertising in European journals is necessary.

For projects over £1 million that require approval above Trust level there is a three-stage business case approval process comprising Strategic Context, Outline Business Case and Full Business Case (*NHS Business Case Guide for Capital Investments*), which follows the general principles discussed above.

PLANNING AND EXECUTION   Once you have secured the financial and physical resources to fund the project you need to establish the organizational structures and control mechanisms to ensure that it is properly executed. There are several elements required to plan and execute any project successfully (Box 8.3).

Box 8.3
Key elements in project planning

> ◆ Clearly defined objectives and constraints – time, quality and cost.
>
> ◆ A project manager with sufficient skills, resources and authority to deliver the objectives.
>
> ◆ A group of senior management and key stakeholders, including clinical end users, overseeing the project manager to monitor progress against plan and ensure that objectives are met.
>
> ◆ A plan which clearly communicates the key tasks, their interdependencies and significant milestones to all.

Figure 8.2 shows a typical organization for a major construction project.

Objectives   The original objectives of the project should be revisited and made more specific, e.g. the original objective may have been to provide the tertiary cardiac service for a particular population, but this may subsequently be defined in more detail to provide 75 beds, 2 catheter laboratories and 3 theatres on a particular site by a fixed date within a set budget. All project objectives are a balance between time, quality and cost. Within the NHS the cost constraint is usually the most emphasized and certainly the most rigorously monitored. By contrast, the time constraint is normally the least emphasized: it is with good reason that the construction

Figure 8.2
Organization for a
major construction
project

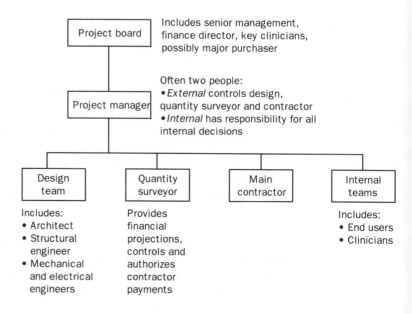

Project board — Includes senior management, finance director, key clinicians, possibly major purchaser

Project manager — Often two people:
- *External* controls design, quantity surveyor and contractor
- *Internal* has responsibility for all internal decisions

Design team
Includes:
- Architect
- Structural engineer
- Mechanical and electrical engineers

Quantity surveyor
Provides financial projections, controls and authorizes contractor payments

Main contractor

Internal teams
Includes:
- End users
- Clinicians

industry's term for a project that appears to have no end is a 'hospital job'.

The project manager

For major projects, it is usual to appoint a project manager who has the responsibility to ensure that the project's objectives are met. The project manager must have sufficient authority to direct the resources necessary to achieve the objectives and must also be relieved of line management responsibilities to enable sufficient time to be given to the role. The project manager must establish procedures, processes and an organization to ensure that:

♦ Quality – all key elements of the design, construction, installation and commissioning meet the needs of the end users.
♦ Time – these decisions and the overall programme meet the time scales specified by the objectives.
♦ Cost – the project remains within budget.

Planning tools

There is a wide variety of techniques to assist with planning, determining critical tasks and communicating the programme. What follows is a review of the most common of these and their advantages.

Many computer programs are available that automate much of the planning process. However, these programs only assist with the manipulation and presentation of the information that is entered. The quality of the input information is vital: 'garbage in, garbage out'. It is much better to use a simple manual technique with transparent logic than fancy software that produces lengthy output of dubious quality. However, in the right hands there is no doubt

Figure 8.3
Bar (Gantt) chart

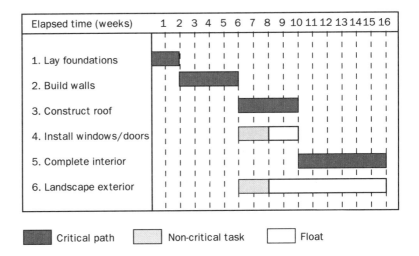

Elapsed time (weeks)	1 2 3 4 5 6 7 8 9 10 11 12 13 14 15 16
1. Lay foundations	
2. Build walls	
3. Construct roof	
4. Install windows/doors	
5. Complete interior	
6. Landscape exterior	

■ Critical path   ▦ Non-critical task   □ Float

that the scheduling and organization of complex projects can be simplified and assisted by computers.

Bar charts (or *Gantt charts*) are the most effective means of communicating a project programme to a wide audience (Figure 8.3 shows a bar chart for a simple construction programme). They are useful in planning simple projects. Bar charts with more than 15 tasks are not likely to be understood by a lay audience and consideration should be given to creating a master programme (bar chart) with subsidiary programmes to detail an individual task or tasks. Even if more sophisticated planning techniques are used, bar charts are the single most effective way of communicating a project plan or progress.

A simple example of *critical path* or *network analysis* is shown in Figure 8.4.

Network analysis deconstructs a project into discrete tasks. Each task is then assessed for:

♦ A time duration, and
♦ Other tasks that must be completed prior to being able to start this task (e.g. 'Lay foundations' must be done before 'Build walls').

When this has been completed for all tasks, it is possible to calculate, either manually or using a computer, the following:

♦ 'Critical path' for the project.
♦ Overall duration of the project.
♦ 'Float time' for each task.
♦ Earliest and latest start and finish times for each task without affecting the overall project duration.

The *critical path* is the sequence of tasks which determine the overall duration of the project (shown in both Figures 8.3 and 8.4).

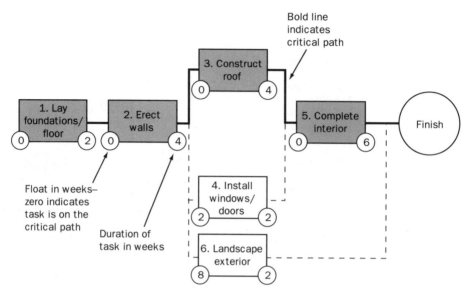

Figure 8.4
Critical path analysis

A delay or acceleration in any one of these tasks will result in an overall delay or acceleration of the entire project. For example, if the roof takes six weeks to complete instead of four, then the project finish date will be delayed by two weeks. Conversely, small delays in tasks not on the critical path will not delay completion. Significant delays in these tasks may, however, change the critical path.

The amount of delay possible without affecting the overall completion date is the *float time*. Zero float time indicates the task is on the critical path. For example, if installing the windows and doors takes three weeks instead of two there would be no effect on the project finish date. However, if they took five weeks (three weeks longer than planned) there would be a delay of one week: the amount by which the float time of two weeks was exceeded. More complex techniques can look at 'resource utilization' and 'resource smoothing'. For example, if a tower crane or a particularly skilled computer programmer is the constraining (and most expensive) resource then all tasks which involve that resource can be identified, quantified and scheduled to ensure optimal *resource utilization*. Altering the timing of tasks to reduce variations in resource utilization is known as *resource smoothing*.

Changing the plan   If it is planned well, the doing should be easy. The doing is never easy! From the objectives (always bear in mind what you are trying to ultimately achieve) decide what aspects of the doing you need to monitor and control closely. This may be progress against plan, costs against budget, quality against specification.

A continual process of reassessment against objectives if you have to make compromises (as you will) is a good discipline as it forces you to decide what is important and what is not. Plans should be seen as dynamic and able to be changed to suit unanticipated developments. With the increasing pace of change in the NHS, flexibility is a necessity and *contingency planning* can help prepare for changes. Contingency planning answers 'what if' questions such as: 'what if the projected workload doubles (or halves)?' This enables the project to anticipate such scenarios and be better prepared should they occur. However, communication of changes in plans to all parties is vital to ensure that everyone is pulling in the same direction.

Global project methodologies   PRINCE (PRojects IN a Controlled Environment) is a comprehensive structured method of project management which has become widely accepted within the NHS. It is mandatory on all information management and technology projects over £1 million. The definitive manuals are in five volumes covering: introduction, technical, management, quality and configuration management. These are not recommended reading, but if an organization is involved in a project using PRINCE, then a reference copy should be available. There are a wide range of training courses and publications available (some are listed in Further Reading).

It is important that PRINCE (or any other formal project management methodology that is used) should not be applied too rigidly. The methodology should not become the objective of the project. PRINCE has a mixed reputation within the NHS, primarily due to misguided application. There is no substitute for staff with sound project management skills.

COMPLETION   The handover of project completion should be defined at the start of project as the realization of the objectives. This is an event rather than an extended activity and is the point at which the project ceases to exist and is handed over to the line organization to be managed on a continuing basis. Formal project completion should also ensure that outstanding issues are identified and assigned to particular individuals for resolution.

EVALUATION   Audit is useful only to the extent that lessons can be learnt (within the organization or elsewhere) for the future. This should determine the significance that audits play. It may be appropriate to limit it to a reconciliation of finances. For certain projects Post Project Evaluation (PPE) is a mandatory NHS requirement.

The next three sections cover specific issues that are frequently encountered in the NHS: managing construction, information technology and organizational change projects.

MANAGING CONSTRUCTION PROJECTS

For major construction projects there are four groups of people involved:

♦ The design team including architects and engineers – structural, electrical, mechanical, public health.
♦ Quantity surveyors, responsible for financial planning and control
♦ Contractors, who organize and construct the building.
♦ Internal users.

Managing and controlling the myriad of internal users and other interested parties is the most difficult and important task of the project manager for a number of reasons:

♦ Internal users are unlikely to be used to a project approach and may not understand the discipline required for a successful outcome.
♦ It is often their only chance to significantly alter their, or their department's, working environment for many years.
♦ There is little incentive for individual users to make the trade-offs between quality, time and cost; they are often competing for resources against other users or departments.
♦ Many people find it difficult to envisage how a building will function at the design stage. An important role of the architect is to communicate the proposed design before it is built in a way that people can understand.

People always want more space than they need. One of the roles of the project manager is to manage people's expectations and negotiate compromises on cost, quality and time. A useful tactic is to get users to consider either/or options: for example, a ward can either have a new case conference room or a new treatment room, but not both. This forces users to start to make trade-offs.

Given the opportunity, people will change their minds many times. The project manager must make clear and communicate to all parties:

♦ Who needs to have input into the design brief.
♦ The dates by which decisions need to be made.
♦ Who the individuals are who need to agree and sign drawings, room data sheets, etc.

It is important for all parties to understand that design is a significant task on the critical path and failure to provide information to the designers by the target dates will delay completion. Design requires significant clinical input to ensure that the building and equipment are suitable for the purpose intended.

Changes prior to appointing the building contractor are cheap and may cause delays. Changes after appointment are always expensive and always cause delays.

Always remember the building or equipment is not an end in itself. If in doubt, return to the original objectives and consider a particular decision in light of these.

INFORMATION TECHNOLOGY PROJECTS

As with any project, it is important to define clearly the objectives in terms of the benefits sought. The successful installation of a new computer system may be the means of achieving these benefits. It is not possible to review information technology (IT) projects here in any depth, but some important points to note are listed in Box 8.4.

Box 8.4
IT projects

- ♦ Ensure all users and suppliers clearly agree the functionality (i.e. a summary of the inputs, outputs and features of the system) required to achieve the benefits.

- ♦ Do not allow creeping extensions to functionality unless the supplier clearly agrees total cost and time impact.

- ♦ Ideally having one supplier responsible for the delivery of the entire information system, its integration with existing systems and training of staff makes lines of accountability more straightforward. This will include supplying and installing hardware (computers, monitors, cabling, printers, etc.), software and training.

- ♦ The introduction of a computer system always involves changing people's behaviour and working practices, for example doctors using a computerized diagnostic coding system rather than coding clerks interpreting manual discharge summaries. A successful implementation will require changes to working practices and may involve loss of certain roles.

- ♦ Training is vital to the success of IT projects. Costs for trainers and to cover for staff to be released to be trained are likely to be significant and must be allowed for.

- ♦ Finally, do not take the projected benefits at face value. IT projects invariably take longer and cost more than originally planned, whilst they rarely fulfil their original intent. Evaluation is difficult and often neglected.

ORGANIZATIONAL CHANGE PROJECTS

In many ways, the management of organizational change is the most difficult project of all. Organizational change is anything which affects:

♦ The jobs staff do – expanding, contracting, creating or eliminating roles. For example nurses giving intravenous therapy or creating a new community liaison post.
♦ The numbers of staff in particular grades or categories.
♦ The relationships between staff, for example the establishment of a surgical clinical directorate making nursing staff managerially responsible to the surgery manager rather than the director of nursing.
♦ Work processes, for example creating a single patient record rather than each profession maintaining separate documents.

Organizational change is often difficult to define and manage as a project as it may not have a fixed end point. For example, one objective of an organizational change project might be to create an organization which is capable of continuous improvement which, by definition, will undergo constant evolution and change in the future. In addition, responsibilities for project and ongoing management are difficult to disentangle, particularly once implementation starts.

Organizational change is more straightforward in the context of a new building or transfer of services from one site to another because there is a physical relocation of staff that necessitates the organizational change. Provided that staff understand the need for physical changes, it is easier for them to accept organizational changes.

In order to succeed, major organizational change in the NHS must have:

♦ Senior management commitment from the Chief Executive and Trust Board.
♦ Clinicians' commitment.
♦ Clinical input into the design and implementation of the changes.

There are two principal approaches to undertaking organizational change (sometimes known in management jargon as *business process re-engineering*). These are 'top down' or 'bottom up'. Successful implementation usually requires a combination of both.

'Top down' organizational change

A top down approach is where senior management designs the changes which will take place without significant contribution from staff in the area affected. This is often used where:

♦ Significant redundancies are anticipated.
♦ Rapid implementation is necessary.
♦ Management do not trust themselves to involve staff. This is a bad reason to use a top down approach as it reflects poor management–staff relationships.

A top down approach has a short design phase as it involves few people in the decision-making process. It also has a significant risk of errors as senior management seldom know enough about the 'coal face' to undertake detailed organization redesign. This makes achieving the objectives during implementation more difficult, as the staff affected will rightly feel that the changes have been imposed with little consultation or involvement. If a top down approach is adopted, then communication with staff should be frequent, open and honest, informing staff of the process, timetable and decisions as soon as possible.

'Bottom up' organizational change   Conversely, a bottom up approach involves staff in the process, takes greater time and effort and extends the design period. This is usually a worthwhile investment as involving more people in the decision-making makes commitment to the changes recommended more likely. It is essential to select staff who have the respect and confidence of their peers, irrespective of their positions in the organization. Care is needed in supporting staff involved in the design to ensure that they are not isolated or ostracized from their peers. A bottom up approach does not reduce the need for Trust management commitment and support. If anything, the need is greater as extending the design period and involving staff gives more time for the project to succumb to second thoughts from within the organization. The Trust management must:

♦ Establish a coherent rationale.
♦ Define the goals.
♦ Ensure adequate resources are available.
♦ Overcome internal resistance to change.

Many institutions both within health care and across many industries, are devolving responsibility further down their organizations and reducing the number of job categories whilst broadening the skills of individuals. A consequence of this is significant role changes and reductions in the number of middle managers (such as sub-department and department heads). This group is often the most threatened by, and resistant to, organizational change. It may be necessary to by-pass these staff in the design phase, but there is no hard and fast rule and staff should be treated on an individual basis.

SUMMARY

♦ A project can be defined as anything that is not part of the regular activity of the hospital which requires specific resourcing. It may involve:
 – Provision of new facilities or equipment.
 – Alteration or introduction of information systems.
 – Significant development or transfer of services.
 – Changes to organization or staff.

♦ All projects should have objectives specified which, when achieved, indicate the end of the project. Overall objectives should be defined in terms of outcomes (quality, service, cost, time to achieve) not means, e.g. a new computer system.

♦ The selection of a particular project requires:
  - The consideration of a range of options including 'do nothing'.
  - Defining appraisal criteria, both economic and non-economic.
  - Assessing each option against the criteria to select the best solution.

♦ An assessment of the risks and sensitivity of options to changes in assumptions is necessary to ensure the project is feasible and robust.

♦ Bar charts are the simplest tool for planning and communicating project timetables. Critical path or network analysis is useful for planning complex projects. Even on complex projects, bar charts are the most widely understood for communicating timetables.

♦ Structured project planning methodologies such as PRINCE can be useful. However, there is no substitute for a good project manager with dedicated time.

♦ In construction projects, the management and control of parties inside the hospital is vital to the overall success. There is the need for a single point of contact (the project manager) and clear timetables for agreeing the design. Late design changes have significant cost and time penalties.

♦ Information technology (IT) projects must have the system functionality (features, inputs and outputs) clearly defined. A single supplier for hardware, software, installation and training can reduce the risk of failure. A successful IT project is one that is being used productively by staff to improve performance, not an installed system being demonstrated by experts. Training is important and entails a significant cost.

♦ Organizational change can be the most difficult project of all and needs both Trust management and clinical commitment. Successful implementation requires senior management support to ensure adequate resources are available and establish the project's rationale and goals. The involvement of staff in the design process is vital to get the best solution and commitment to changes recommended.

FURTHER READING

♦ Bentley, C. (1992), *Introducing Prince, The Structured Project Management Method*, NCC/Blackwell, Manchester/Oxford.

♦ Hammer M. and Champy, J. (1993) *Re-engineering the Corporation.* Nicholas Brearly Publishing, London.

A good general text on successfully implementing organizational change.

♦ Meredith, J. R. and Mantel, S. J. (1989), *Project Management – A Managerial Approach*, 2nd edn, Wiley, Chichester.

A general, comprehensive reference text.

♦ NHS IMGME (1993), *Investment Appraisal and Benefits Realisation for Information Management and Technology in the NHS*, IMGME, Leeds.

The NHS manual for IT project approval.

♦ NHSME (1994), *NHS Business Case Guide for Capital Investments*, NHSME, Leeds.

The NHS manual for capital project approval.

♦ Turner, J. R. (1993), *The Handbook of Project Based Management*, McGraw-Hill, London.

A general, comprehensive reference text.

EVALUATION OF CLINICAL SERVICES

Anthony J. Newman Taylor and William Bain

CHAPTER 9

OBJECTIVES

♦ To appraise critically the techniques available for the evaluation of both diagnostic and therapeutic clinical services and their cost-effectiveness.

♦ To demonstrate the relevance of the principles on which these techniques are based to the clinician making choices about the allocation of resources to different services.

INTRODUCTION

I asked a worker at a crematorium, who had a curiously contented look on his face, what he found so satisfying about his work. He replied that what fascinated him was the way so much went in and so little came out. I thought of advising him to get a job in the NHS. (Cochrane, 1972)

In an editorial in the *New England Journal of Medicine*, Relman (1988) distinguished three phases in medical care delivery since World War II in the United States: the 'Era of Expansion', the 'Era of Cost Containment' (or 'Revolt of the Payers') and the contemporary 'Era of Assessment and Accountability'. The era of expansion, which started in the late 1940s and lasted through the 1960s, was characterized by 'rapid growth in hospital facilities and the number of physicians and new developments in science and technology. Medical schools increased and produced an army of new specialists trained in the use of sophisticated technology'. It could be described as an era of optimism when enormous resources were invested in medical care and research in the belief that if some was good, more would be better. Unsurprisingly, payers (including governments) expressed increasing concern about the rapidly rising costs of medical care. The subsequent era of cost containment was characterized by the institution of cost control through systems such as payment of diagnosis related groups (DRGs). Disquiet about cost has been compounded by lack of evidence that increased costs are demonstrably associated with benefit, as shown by the wide geographical variations in the levels of service provision which appear unrelated to variation in the incidence of disease or differences in outcome. The recognition that the necessarily limited resources available for health care must be used in the most cost-effective way to obtain maximum value in terms of 'health gain' has heralded the contemporary era of assessment and accountability.

This chapter will focus on the means of evaluating clinical services including the resource implications of existing and new services and techniques for evaluating 'gain' from clinical services both diagnostic and therapeutic.

INTRODUCTION OF NEW SERVICES   Clinical services, including the introduction of new diagnostic procedures and treatments (both medical and surgical), develop continuously but have to be introduced within finite resources. One approach to this dilemma is to introduce new services only after evaluation of their clinical and economic impact. To do this an 'impact analysis' can be undertaken which asks sponsors of new clinical services to identify:

◆ The purpose of the new service.
◆ The resource implications – including space, staff, equipment and other costs.
◆ The 'impact' that the introduction of the new programme/ service would have on other departments (for example, will the new programme require additional laboratory tests, additional imaging procedures, etc?). Note: These other department heads should sign the Impact Analysis to indicate their agreement with the implication for their department.
◆ Identification of services/programmes it may replace or reduce demand for.
◆ Identification of the priority of the sponsoring department.
◆ The benefits to be derived.

A similar approach has been suggested for the introduction of new high cost, low volume drugs such as erythropoietin and DNase and diagnostic and therapeutic devices (Rawlins, 1993). Before their introduction, sponsors are asked to identify:

◆ *Benefit*:
   – Clinical benefits – efficacy and safety – and comparison with current alternative treatments.
   – Assessment of effect on survival and quality of life.
◆ *Costs* of new treatment for different groups of patients in whom it is indicated:
   1. Direct drug costs.
   2. Indirect non-drug costs (e.g. additional investigations such as plasma drug level measurements, and hospital attendance/ admission).
   3. Compensatory drug and non-drug savings.

◆ *Patients who will benefit.* Identification of groups of patients likely to benefit with ordered assessment of level of benefit.

Impact analysis ensures the provision of quantitative information and compels proponents of a new service or drug to examine benefits claimed in relation to existing services or interventions. The approach allows economic analysis of the proposed change through evaluation of the marginal benefits and costs in relation to current practice. The new service or drug should be introduced when its marginal cost-effectiveness is demonstrably superior to the old (see section on evaluating and clinical services, below).

OUTCOMES   The purpose of medical services in hospital and in the community is to extend life and improve its quality ('health gain'). Resources provided for health care vary considerably between different countries, but all require choices to be made between competing demands. Demographic changes and the continuous development and introduction of new and expensive technologies mean that such choices must now be made more explicitly. Ideally, scarce resources should be allocated to maximize improvement in health gain; failure to maximize health gain most efficiently may be considered unethical as it deprives other patients of potential benefit. This requires knowledge of the outcomes of medical interventions – both diagnostic and therapeutic – and their costs. This implies evaluation of what works (to improve survival and quality of life), what is valued by patients and the cost of achieving this (i.e. the opportunity cost – the improvement in health that others will have to forgo if resources are used in a particular way).

The consequences of lack of knowledge of outcomes are considerable and are reflected in the variation in medical practice observed in different areas of similar demographic and socio-economic status – a mismatch between epidemiology of disease and the epidemiology of health care. For example, the number of beds per head of population in 1982 was found to be some 55% greater in Boston than New Haven, two cities which were demographically similar with hospital care provided predominantly by university hospitals (Wennberg, Freeman and Culp, 1987). Admission rates for conditions for which there is a large measure of agreement between doctors on the need for hospitalization (such as myocardial infarction) were similar. The majority of increased bed provision in Boston was used for elective admissions for common acute medical conditions where agreement does not exist, such as back problems, gastroenteritis, heart failure, uncomplicated pneumonia and diabetes. Variation in major surgical procedures were also observed: patients in New Haven were about twice as likely to have coronary artery bypass grafts (CABG) for coronary heart disease, whereas patients in Boston were more likely to be treated medically; patients in Boston were substantially more likely to have knee and hip prostheses than patients in New Haven whose doctors preferred conservative treatment. At least in part these differences reflect insufficient knowledge of the outcome of different treatment to guide practice. The cost consequences were considerable; application of the costs of care for the residents of Boston in 1982 to the rest of the USA would have consumed 16% of the US gross national product whereas application of the costs of health care incurred by the residents of New Haven would have consumed only 9%. Interestingly, readmission rates during three years of follow-up for five conditions where agreement on the need for initial hospitalization has been found to be high – acute myocardial infarction, acute gastrointestinal bleeding, fracture of hip, curative surgery for cancer of breast, colon or lung – were 64% higher in Boston than New Haven, independent of age, sex and ethnic group (Fisher, 1994). Mortality rates during the first 30 days after discharge and the three year period of the study, were not different, making it unlikely the different readmission rates reflected differences in case mix severity.

The means of knowing what works in health care has been the randomized controlled clinical trial which, through the work in the 1940s by Bradford Hill, brought the experimental approach into clinical medicine. The experimental design of the clinical trial with random allocation and blind (or masked) observations ensures a high degree of 'internal validity', minimizing the risk of unsuspected confounding bias. More than 20 years ago Cochrane argued strongly that the results of randomized controlled trials (RCTs) should provide the basis for making choices in the National Health Service and recommended the annual award of a 'Bradford' to the best medical statistical paper of the year (Cochrane, 1972). However, RCTs have their limitations. They are constrained by the patients suitable and available for the study who are willing to participate; this can cause serious limitations in generalization from the results of the study (limiting 'external validity'). Because of strict selection criteria for inclusion it has been estimated that the results of the many studies of coronary artery bypass surgery do not apply to some 90% of patients in whom this procedure is currently undertaken. RCTs are also expensive and time consuming and not all clinically important questions can be investigated by them. To overcome these difficulties and provide data on the effectiveness of treatment provision, observational studies have been undertaken of the outcomes of treatment in hospitals using routinely acquired data. Such studies suffer the limitations of all observational investigations, in particular their ability to compare 'like with like' and to separate the effects of specific interventions from other potentially confounding influences on outcome such as case mix severity, coexisting conditions (comorbidity) and demographic factors such as age and socio-economic status. While some of these factors, where specified, can be allowed for in analysis, unrecognized confounders, such as the reasons different doctors prefer one treatment to another, cannot.

A study comparing the outcomes of open prostatectomy and transurethral prostatectomy (TURP), using routinely acquired data from hospitals in Denmark, England and Canada, highlights the difficulties in interpreting such observational findings. Age specific mortality rates during the five years after operation in patients without evidence at operation of bladder or prostate cancer was 45% higher after TURP than open prostatectomy. Mortality remained similarly increased after adjustment for comorbidity identified in the Canadian study population, with a 2.5 greater risk of dying of acute myocardial infarction after TURP than after open prostatectomy (Roos *et al.*, 1989). In a subsequent study of men in New Haven, comparing five year mortality rates after TURP and open prostatectomy for benign prostatic hyperplasia using hospital records rather than routinely acquired statistics, Concato *et al.* (1992) found that while the crude five year mortality rates were 17.5% after TURP and 13.5% after open prostatectomy, after adjustment for age and comorbid conditions, there was no difference in mortality rates. The authors highlighted the problem of identifying relevant coexisting disease from data routinely acquired for administrative purposes – the main data source in the first study – which was available from clinical information recorded in medical records.

Despite the difficulties and the different limitations of these two experimental and observational studies, choices and decisions made by practising clinicians and purchasers of health care will increasingly be informed by their results. Medical practice based upon the results of scientific studies including meta-analyses has been called in North America 'evidence based medicine' and its proponents have published methods to help clinicians identify and evaluate the relevant scientific literature (Evidence Based Medicine Working Group, 1992). Two methods, the use of likelihood ratios in interpreting the result of a diagnostic test and the use of 'number needed to treat', in the interpretation of the benefits and risks of treatment, are particularly suited to informing clinicians of the 'gain' to be anticipated from a diagnostic test and a therapeutic intervention.

Diagnostic gain:
Likelihood ratios

An ideal diagnostic test would provide the clinician with an unequivocal statement as to the presence or absence of a particular disease. In reality, very few results achieve this and the majority simply increase or reduce the probability of the presence of a particular disease in an individual. The starting point of a diagnostic process is the findings from the history and clinical examination, which provides a pre-test (or prior) probability of the presence of a disease. The results of diagnostic tests modify the pre-test probability of the disease to provide a new post-test probability. This in turn becomes a pre-test probability which may again be modified by the result of other tests to provide a further post-test probability. Diagnostic tests should be undertaken when the result will influence clinical action. Cochrane (1972) provided characteristically simple advice about the use of diagnostic tests: 'Before ordering a test, decide what you will do if it is (a) positive, and (b) negative, and if both answers are the same, don't do the test.'

The value of a diagnostic test is determined by the accuracy with which it identifies a disease. The measures of accuracy most commonly used are its sensitivity (the proportion of those with the disease who have a positive test) and specificity (the proportion of those without the disease in whom the test is negative) (Box 9.1). With the exception of wholly specific tests (which have no false positives, when a positive test is diagnostic) and wholly sensitive tests (which have no false negatives when a negative test excludes the diagnosis), knowledge of the sensitivity and specificity of a test is of limited value because the clinician is not concerned with the proportion of those with the disease in whom the test is positive, but the proportion of those with a positive test who have the disease. This is the predictive value of the test, whose value is dependent on the prevalence of the disease. Positive predictive value (the proportion of those with a positive test who have the disease) falls as disease prevalence falls and the number of false positives increase. Because the predictive value of a test depends upon the prevalence of the disease in the population tested it will usually fall from hospital to general practice to the community, a consequence which has reduced the value of several diagnostic tests with a high predictive value in hospital patients as screening tests in the community.

A more clinically useful measure of accuracy of a test is the likelihood ratio, which is the ratio of the proportion of those with a positive test who have the disease to those with a positive test who do not have the disease (the ratio of the true positive rate to the false positive rate). Unlike the predictive value, the likelihood ratio

Box 9.1
The 'truth' and the test

	'Truth' (gold standard for disorder)	
	Present	*Absent*
Positive	True positive (TP)	False positive (FP)
Test		
Negative	False negative (FN)	True negative (TN)

Sensitivity = TP/(TP + FN)
Specificity = TN/(TN + FP)
Positive predictive value   TP/(TP + FP)
Likelihood ratio   [TP/(TP + FN)]/[FP/(FP + TN)]

Box 9.2
Diagnostic tests and
likelihood ratios

$$\text{Odds} = \text{probability}/1 - \text{probability} = P/1 - P$$

i.e. where P = 80%

$$\text{Odds} = 0.8/0.2 = 4\!:\!1$$

where P = 50%

$$\text{Odds} = 0.5/0.5 = 1\!:\!1$$

where P = 20%

$$\text{Odds} = 0.2/0.8 = 0.25\!:\!1$$

$$\text{Probability} = \text{odds}/1 + \text{odds}$$

i.e. where odds = 4:1

$$P = 4/5 = 0.8 = 80\%$$

$$\text{Pre-test odds} \times \text{likelihood ratio} = \text{post-test odds}$$

is not affected by disease prevalence. Results from hospital practice are therefore applicable to general practice. To use likelihood ratios probabilities have to be converted to odds and vice versa (Box 9.2). Multiplication of the likelihood ratio by the pre-test odds of the disease being present provides the post-test odds of the disease being present given a positive test result. The value of likelihood ratios in changing pre- to post-test odds (and probabilities) is shown in Box 9.3.

Box 9.3
Interpretation of
likelihood ratios

Likelihood ratios		Change from pre- to post-test probability
>10	<1	Large, often decisive
5–10	0.1–0.2	Moderate
1–5	0.5–1	Small (although sometimes important)

In the examples (Boxes 9.4 and 9.5) the sensitivity and specificity of an abnormal liver scan for liver disease is 0.8 and 0.63 in both patient groups (Altman, 1991). Because the prevalence of the disease in the first group is 75% (Box 9.4) and in the second group 25% (Box 9.5) the positive predictive value of a positive test falls from 88% in the first group to 45% in the second group. The likelihood ratio is the same because the true positive rate and false positive rate are the same in both groups. In the first group (Box 9.4) the disease prevalence is 75% and the pre-test odds of the disease is 0.75/0.25 = 3; in the second group the disease prevalence is 25% and the pre-test odds is 0.25/0.75 = 0.33 (Box 9.5).

Box 9.4
Liver disease

		Present	Absent	
Liver	*Abnormal*	231	32	263
Scan	*Normal*	27	54	81
		258	86	344

Sensitivity = 231/258 = 0.9
Specificity = 54/86 = 0.63
Disease prevalence = 258/344 = 0.75

Positive predictive
value = 231/263
= 0.88

Negative predictive
value = 54/81
= 0.67

Likelihood ratio = [(231/258)/(32/86)]/[0.895/0.372]
= 2.4

Worked from examples in
Altman (1991)

Box 9.5
Liver disease

		Present	Absent	
Liver	*Abnormal*	77	96	173
Scan	*Normal*	9	162	171
		86	258	344

Sensitivity = 77/868 = 0.9
Specificity = 162/258 = 0.63
Disease prevalence = 86/344 = 0.25

Positive predictive
value = 77/173
= 0.45

Negative predictive
value = 162/171
= 0.95

Likelihood ratio = [(77/86)/(96/258)]/[0.895/0.372]
= 2.4

Worked from examples in
Altman (1991)

Pre-test odds × likelihood ratio = post-test odds.

For Group 1 (Box 9.4):

$$3 \times 2.4 = 7.2$$

Therefore post-test probability = 7.2/8.2 = 0.88.
For Group 2 (Box 9.5):

$$0.33 \times 2.4 = 0.792$$

Therefore post-test probability = 0.792/1.792 = 0.44.

The probability of having liver disease with an abnormal scan is therefore 88% in the first group of patients, and 44% in the second. The diagnostic gain (increase from pre- to post-test probability) in the first group was $88 - 75\% = 13\%$ and in the second group $44 - 25\% = 19\%$.

Likelihood ratios are being estimated for an increasing number of diagnostic tests; they seem likely in the future to become an important characteristic of a test allowing the diagnostic gain of a positive test in a particular patient to be quantified in the light of an estimate of the pre-test probability of the disease.

Therapeutic gain: Number needed to treat

The effect of treatment on a disease is dependent on (1) the absolute risk of a particular outcome – death or particular complications (such as a myocardial infarction or stroke in patients with hypertension, and (2) the relative reduction in the risk of the outcome provided by the treatment. A treatment which provides 25% reduction in the risk of death in one year has a different value if the absolute risk in the untreated is 10% (which is reduced to 7.5%) or 1% (which is reduced to 0.75%). This difference is expressed in the absolute risk reduction which in the first case is 2.5% (0.025) and in the second case is 0.25% (0.0025). The reciprocal of the absolute risk reduction is the number needed to treat (to prevent one death in one year in this example) which in the first case would be $1/0.025 = 40$ and in the second $1/0.0025 = 400$. A similar strategy can be used to enumerate the risk of adverse events and analyse the benefits and costs of different treatments as the number of adverse events caused, per number of deaths or complications prevented.

In the example (Box 9.6), although the relative risk reduction of antihypertensive treatment was similar in those with and without prior organ damage, the absolute risk reduction was more than twice as great in those with prior organ damage. The number needed to treat to prevent one major complication was correspondingly less, and the pay off (or potential for benefit) from treatment more than twice as great in those with prior organ damage than in those without (Lapaucis, Sackett and Roberts, 1988).

Box 9.6
Occurrence of stroke or other major complication in antihypertensive men on active treatment and placebo
After Lapaucis *et al.* (1988) using data from Veterans Administrative Cooperative Study Group on Antihypertensive Agents.

Patient status at entry	Adverse events		Relative risk reduction (RRR) $(P - A)/P$	Absolute risk reduction (ARR) $P - A$	Number needed to treat $(1/ARR)$
	Placebo (P)	Active (A)			
Prior organ damage	0.22	0.08	64%	0.14	7
No prior organ damage	0.10	0.04	60%	0.06	17

AUDIT   Audit has been often and variously defined. Probably the most widely cited definition is that of the 1989 White Paper: 'the systematic critical analysis of the quality of medical care, including the procedures used for diagnosis and treatment, the use of resources and the resulting outcome and quality of life for the patient'. This definition describes the subject matter of audit, but Crombie *et al.* (1993) have challenged it as 'singularly unhelpful because it failed to identify the purposes of audit or suggest how studies should be carried out'. They proposed as an alternative: 'audit is the process of reviewing the delivery of health care to identify deficiencies so that they may be remedied'. It would seem fruitless to offer further definitions of audit, but an appreciation of its purpose is probably worthwhile. Audit is concerned with the quality of the delivery of health care – 'doing things right'. Healthcare delivery has several dimensions which have been divided into structure (what facilities are there?), process (what was done to the patient?) and outcome (what was the result?) (Figure 9.1). Clearly, the most important issue for the patient is a successful outcome and ideally audit should focus on whether the benefits expected of treatment were achieved and whether any adverse effects occurred. Unfortunately, satisfactory methods to measure outcome are available for only a minority of interventions, primarily procedures, and even in these circumstances adverse events (particularly mortality) are easier to quantify than the benefits of treatment. For this reason many analyses of the quality of healthcare delivery have examined what was done (process) rather than its outcome, with the emphasis on the easily

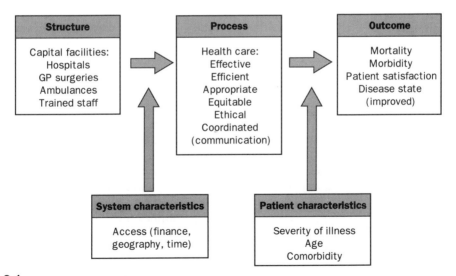

Figure 9.1
Dimensions of healthcare delivery

After Hopkins (1994)

Figure 9.2
The audit cycle

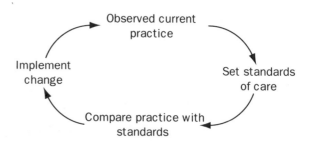

measurable, such as waiting lists for appointments and operations, length of waiting times in outpatients and frequency of cancelled operations.

Whatever is audited needs a basis for comparison, commonly a standard against which current practice can be assessed. This is the basis of the widely accepted 'audit cycle' (Figure 9.2).

The source of an appropriate standard of care may be internal and potentially arbitrary (e.g. wound infections after thoracotomy should be less than 5%) or increasingly commonly, an external standard, such as nationally agreed guidelines (e.g. British Thoracic Society guidelines for the management of asthma). A commonly reported failing of audit is the lack of subsequent change: it is easier to identify problems than to solve them. Where changes have been implemented, examination of their effectiveness by completing the cycle is undertaken infrequently.

As discussed earlier, indices of outcome need to be considered in the context of measurement of case mix severity; for comparisons to be informative like must be compared with like. Relevant patient characteristics include disease severity, comorbidity (e.g. diabetes, hypertension) and age. These patient characteristics are included in an index of case severity used in the assessment of outcome of cardiac surgery, the Parsonnet score, measured as death rate within 30 days of operation (Parsonnet, Dean and Bernstein, 1989). The Parsonnet score provides both a 'predicted mortality' in relation to case mix severity and a basis for comparison between different institutions. The score incorporates, in an additive model, scores for disease severity (including measures of left ventricular function and reoperation), comorbidity (obesity, hypertension, diabetes) and age. The relationship of 30 day postoperative mortality for all cardiac operations at Royal Brompton Hospital to Parsonnet score in comparison both to predicted and published data from Wythenshawe Hospital (Samer *et al.*, 1992) is shown in Box 9.7. There is a linear relationship with Parsonnet score in the results from both hospitals which are similar and in general better than 'predicted'.

Audit has several benefits: it allows identification of shortcomings in the delivery of care and evaluation of the effectiveness of the methods used to improve them; in achieving this it has considerable educational value; it will also increasingly be of value to organizations who need to demonstrate the quality of the health

Box 9.7
A comparison of mortality rate by Parsonnet risk group for Wythenshawe Hospital, Manchester, and RBNH & L for all procedures

Parsonnet risk group	Wythenshawe Hospital			RBNH & L Hospital		
	% of Sample	Actual % mortality	Predicted % mortality	% of Sample	Actual % mortality	Predicted % mortality
Good (0–4)	53.3	1.2 (7/571)	1.4	47.1	0.59 (3/504)	1.4
Fair (5–9)	23.4	4.0 (10/251)	6.3	24.0	0.39 (1/257)	6.7
Poor (10–14)	15.1	6.2 (10/162)	11.8	15.0	4.34 (7/161)	11.5
High (15–19)	4.6	6.1 (3/49)	16.8	8.9	13.54 (13/96)	16.3
Extremely High (20+)	3.5	15.8 (6/38)	29.5	4.9	22.64 (12/53)	24.0
TOTAL		3.4 (36/1071)			3.4 (36/1071)	

Wythenshawe data from Samer *et al.* (1992).

care they provide to their purchasers who in turn are increasingly likely to demand the evidence for this.

EVALUATING CLINICAL SERVICES Appreciation of the need to allocate the limited resources available to health care to achieve maximum benefit is probably the characteristic of the 'era of assessment and accountability' distinguishing it from the 'era of cost-containment' where the concern was to limit expenditure with little consideration for lost benefits. Economic evaluation techniques have been developed to provide a rational basis for making choices between competing demands for the limited resources available. Economic analyses have two characteristics: they are concerned with choices and are therefore comparative; and they include both the costs and consequences (or outcomes) of the activities being evaluated. These characteristics distinguish economic rather than other types of analysis (Box 9.8) and have led to a definition of economic evaluation as the comparative analysis of alternative courses of action in terms of both their costs and their consequences.

There are four types of economic evaluation (Box 9.9).

Box 9.8
Economic analyses

		Analysis of both costs and consequences		
		No		Yes
		Consequences only	Costs only	
Comparison	No	Outcome description	Cost description	Cost outcome description
	Yes	Efficacy or effectiveness evaluation (randomized control trials)	Cost analysis	Economic evaluation: Cost minimization Cost-effectiveness Cost benefit Cost utility

Box 9.9
Types of economic
evaluation

1. Cost-minimization analysis which costs the alternatives and assumes their outcomes are identical.

2. Cost-effectiveness analysis which costs the alternatives and measures the outcomes in common units, e.g. years of life gained.

3. Cost-benefit analysis which values and measures all costs and benefits in financial terms (how is pain avoidance valued in financial terms?).

4. Cost-utility analysis which costs the alternatives and estimates benefit with an outcome measure which is valid for different disease and therapeutic categories, e.g. quality adjusted life year (QALY) and health year equivalents (HYE), which measure the capacity of an intervention to improve both the length and quality of life.

Two important concepts of economic analyses of value in evaluating clinical services are worth emphasis: opportunity costs and marginal analysis. Economists view costs not in financial terms, but as a sacrifice – the benefits given up in the best alternative use of the resources, so-called opportunity cost ('guns or butter' or, as a possible medical analogy 'hearts or hips'). In fact choices are not made between one service or another, but to existing levels of service, whether to increase, reduce or maintain. The costs and benefits associated with these changes are termed 'marginal costs' and 'marginal benefits'. Marginal or incremental benefits should at least equal the marginal costs: if marginal benefits exceed marginal costs then further benefit can be obtained by expansion of the service; if marginal costs exceed marginal benefits then expansion of the service would be associated with a net loss.

These principles were applied by Williams (1985) in a cost utility analysis of coronary artery bypass grafting. He found the costs per QALY gained by coronary artery bypass grafting (CABG) were relatively low for cases of severe angina, left main stem and three vessel disease, but rose sharply for single and double vessel disease. Hip replacement, pacemaker insertion for atrioventricular block and aortic valve replacement were more cost-effective than for CABG for severe angina, left main stem and three vessel disease while treatment of end stage renal failure by haemodialysis was considerably less cost-effective. Williams concluded that:

> *Resources need to be deployed at the margin to procedures for which the benefits to patients are high in relation to the costs, such as the insertion of pacemakers for heart block, hip replacement, replacement of valves for aortic stenosis, and coronary artery*

bypass grafting for severe angina with left main disease and triple vessel disease and moderate angina with left main disease. These treatments should take priority over additional facilities for patients needing kidney transplants and coronary artery bypass grafting for mild angina with left main disease, moderate angina with triple vessel disease, or one vessel disease, and severe angina with one vessel disease, for which costs per quality adjusted life year gained are higher.

A further instructive example comes from a study of marginal costs and benefits of screening the general population, aged more than 40 years, for colonic cancer by testing of six sequential stools for occult blood, as had been recommended by the American Cancer Society (Neuhauser and Lewicki, 1975). Using the results of a previous study, the authors assumed a prevalence rate of 72 per 10 000 population, a true positive rate of 92% for each test and a false positive rate of 36.5%. The first stool examination identified 66 of the 72 cases and the second test a further 5.4 cases (a total 71.4 cases – 99.3%). The subsequent four tests identified the further 0.6 cases with a steadily increasing proportion of false positive test results. Taking a cost of $4 for the first stool examination, $1 for each subsequent examination and $100 for a barium enema undertaken on each person screened with a positive test, the average cost (total cost/number of cases of cancer detected) increased a little from $1175 for the first test to $2451 for the sixth test. However, the marginal cost (cost per case detected by each test) increased dramatically from $1175 for the first test to $47 107 241 for the sixth test – an engaging prospect for consideration of opportunity cost!

CONCLUSION

Few medical staff will be able to undertake formal economic evaluations, but the principles of opportunity cost and of marginal analysis and the methods used in the four different types of study can be valuable guides when making choices between allocation of resources into different services.

SUMMARY

♦ Increasing emphasis in clinical practice is being placed on 'evidence-based' health care and evidence of value for money to provide maximum health gain.

♦ A number of readily applicable methods have been developed which allow the evaluation of diagnostic tests, therapeutic interventions and economic comparisons. These include likelihood ratios to determine the diagnostic gain from a test, number needed to treat to analyse the therapeutic gain from an intervention, and cost effectiveness and cost-utility analyses to determine relative economic efficiency.

♦ The widespread introduction of clinical audit has provided the stimulus to evaluate local standards of clinical practice, with an increasing emphasis on outcomes.

♦ Application of these approaches will help clinicians to improve the effectiveness of their clinical practice and optimize their use of resources.

FURTHER READING

♦ Cochrane, A. (1972), *Effectiveness and Efficiency*, Nuffield Provincial Hospitals Trust.

♦ Tunbridge, M. (Ed.) (1993), *Rationing of Health Care in Medicine*, Royal College of Physicians of London.

♦ Sackett, D. L., Haynes, R. B., Guyatt, G. H. and Tugwell, P. (1991), *Clinical Epidemiology*, 2nd edn, Little Brown & Co., Boston.

REFERENCES

Altman, D. G. (1991), *Practical Statistics for Medical Research.* London: Chapman & Hall.

Cochrane, A. (1972), *Effectiveness and Efficiency.* Nuffield Provincial Hospitals Trust.

Concato, J., Horwitz, R. I., Fenstein, A. R., Elmore, J. G. and Schiff, S. F. (1992), Problems of co-morbidity in mortality after prostatectomy. *Journal of the American Medical Association*, **267**: 1077–1082.

Crombie, I. K., Davies, T. O., Abraham, S. C. S. and Florey, C. D. V. In: *The Audit Handbook 1993.* Chichester: John Wiley.

Evidence Based Medicine Working Group. (1992), Evidence based medicine. A new approach to teaching practice of medicine. *Journal of the American Medical Association*, **268**: 2420–2425.

Fisher, E. S., Wennberg, J. E., Stukel, T. A. and Sharp, S. M. (1994), Hospital readmission rates for cohorts of Medicare beneficiaries in Boston and New Haven. *New England Journal of Medicine*, **331**, 989–995.

Hopkins, A. (1994), In: *Regulation of the market in National Health Service.* London: Royal College of Physicians of London.

Lapaucis, A., Sackett, D. L. and Roberts, R. S. (1988), An assessment of clinically useful measures of the consequences of treatment. *New England Journal of Medicine*, **318**: 1728-1733.

Neuhauser, D. and Lewicki, A. M. (1975), What do we gain from the sixth stool guar. *New England Journal of Medicine*, **293**: 226-228.

Parsonnet, V., Dean, D. and Bernstein, A. D. (1989), A method of uniform stratification of risk for evaluating the result of surgery in acquired adult heart disease. *Circulation*; **79**:suppl I: 3-12.

Rawlins, M. D. (1993), New drugs for old. In: Tunbridge, (Ed.) *Rationing of Health Care in Medicine*. London: Royal College of Physicians of London.

Relman, A. S. (1988), Assessment and accountability. *New England Journal of Medicine*, **319**: 1220-1222.

Roos, N. P., Wennberg, J. E., Malenka, D. J. *et al.* (1989), Mortality and reoperation rate after open and transurethral resection of the prostate for benign prostatic hyperplasia. *New England Journal of Medicine*, **320**: 1120-1124.

Samer, A. M., Carey, F., Silcock, M. M. *et al.* (1992), Trial of the Parsonnet system in a British hospital. *British Medical Journal*, **305**: 1066-1067.

Wennberg, J. E., Freeman, J. J. and Culp, W. J. (1987), Are hospital services rationed in New Haven or over utilised in Boston? *Lancet*, **i**: 1185-1189.

Williams, A. (1985), Economics of coronary artery bypass grafting. *British Medical Journal*, **249**: 326-329.

LIMITS TO CLINICAL MANAGEMENT RESPONSIBILITY

CHAPTER 10

Colin L. Smith

OBJECTIVES

♦ To identify the type of ethical conflicts which can develop between the clinical priorities of the doctor and the contractual commitments of the Trust.

♦ To examine the areas of a clinical manager's responsibility in which these conflicts can arise.

♦ To suggest ways in which intervention by the clinical manager can help resolve these conflicts.

INTRODUCTION

The clinical directorate system was first introduced into England in 1985–86 at Guy's Hospital and Southampton General Hospital. The directorate system essentially followed the principles of clinical services management developed at the Johns Hopkins Hospital, Baltimore, and included a doctor as the director with responsibility for staffing, budget management and the delivery of patient services. As a consequence of the introduction of directorates, responsibility was clearly devolved to clinical directors for leading and managing the service and with it, the quality of patient care. This change also saw a trend towards professional line management often accompanied by the disappearance of the nursing management hierarchy with the employment and distribution of nurses resting ultimately with the clinical director. Responsibility for the professional aspects of nursing remains with a director of nursing. For medical staff, accustomed to a medical executive (without real authority), or a district manager whose control of budgets, staffing and services was, at best, tenuous, there has been a shift to a service-based authority controlled by the clinical director.

There has been an undoubted downward shift of responsibility and accountability for all resource management to the clinical director, yet the limits of their responsibilities have not been, in most instances, clearly set out. Indeed, there are many instances where the clinical director has no budgetary control, where there are independent nursing and administrative structures and yet the director has responsibility and accountability for the service delivery, an arrangement which either is doomed to fail, or barely functions.

A clinical director should therefore have clearly defined responsibilities for budget control, all staffing, non-staff expenditure and contract arrangements within the directorate, with ultimate accountability to the chief executive. Given that, for the majority, being a clinical director will be only a part of a consultant's activities, it is inevitable that there will be areas where there is a conflict between the need to fulfil the service contracts and the clinical role as a consultant constrained by those same service contracts. Potentially the most difficult areas are:

1. the responsibility to provide patient care against the restraints of funding;
2. the inability to develop a service for patients without an appropriate contract;
3. the perceived constraint of clinical freedom; and, perhaps most testing of all,
4. the disciplining or restriction of colleagues who either fail to fulfil their contracts, or whose clinical judgement is questioned.

The changes in the last few years have seen the apparent conflict of business ethics with medical ethics, by which most mean the introduction of commercialism and markets into medical practice. The conflict of these two is not inevitable, but the main concern is the apparent distortion of medical practice by contract arrangements which give priority for care by contract and not by clinical need.

There has always been prioritization or rationing based on waiting lists, determined by urgency of need. The side-stepping of clinically led priorities by a range of contracts with purchasers, together with waiting list initiatives, which of necessity distort prioritization, has created one of the most difficult areas of conflict for any clinical manager, be they medical director of the Trust or a clinical director. The changes in the NHS have, without doubt, sharpened the accountability of all medical professionals, not least consultants, and devolved the responsibility for performance to individual doctors. It is the role of the clinical director to ensure that everyone in the directorate works to the same end.

This chapter will address some of the problems of the responsibilities of clinical directors and the limits within which they work.

The areas to be covered are:

♦ Strategic business planning.
♦ Annual business planning and budget setting.

♦ Budget control.
♦ Staff performance review and discipline.
♦ Quality assurance and complaints.
♦ Education, research and development.
♦ External relationships.

STRATEGIC
BUSINESS
PLANNING

All organizations need a long-term strategic plan which identifies the activities for the next three to five years. Within such a strategic plan, the changes and developments in the organization should be identified as well as the basic programme of services and activities. For a directorate, such plans must conform to the strategic plan for the Trust or hospital. This can give the directorate opportunities for development, or the maintenance of a position, but may sometimes be perceived as a threat in the future.

For example, if the strategic plan for a Trust includes the development of transplantation services, this becomes a major opportunity for the medicine and surgery directorates. Within it, however, may lie a threat, given that funding and space are constrained, such that another service has to be reduced to accommodate the new activity. Given the current funding constraints, many, if not all, developments have to come from within existing resources. Thus, there is an immediate conflict between the business ethic of increasing and expanding the organization at the expense of the less secure, against the medical ethic of providing patient care to all determined by need, with the only constraint being the skills of the practitioner. The pattern of development until now has largely been by addition and expansion. With the introduction of business methods, there are increasing pressures to change practices or to change contracts for services.

The 'threat' will be seen mainly in the need to change practice, which may have been the same for many years, with all the attendant threats to professional pride and the much vaunted 'clinical freedom'. At worst, there will be the real threat to continued employment. From this arises the responsibility of the clinical director to ensure the continuation of contracts and when these are threatened by poor performance, to develop a strategic plan, not only as an immediate remedy, but for long-term reorganization of the threatened service to fulfil new needs.

Within the strategic plan, therefore, there is the requirement for an assessment of the areas of (relative) failure. For example, a rheumatology service which has clinics in both the main and peripheral hospitals has long waiting lists for appointments approaching 40 weeks, yet already individual consultants see an apparently very large number of both new and old patients at both clinics. However, general practitioners, particularly fundholders, are critical of the number of clinics cancelled at the peripheral hospitals. The threat is that the GP fundholders will remove their contracts and place them with a nearby Trust.

An analysis of the data shows several problems.

The consultants all work very hard to try to meet the demand but all have a very high follow-up (or review) workload. The ratio is one new to every six follow-up patients. The follow-up ratio is based on the view that with such chronic disorders, regular follow-up is necessary to avert disease progression and monitor medication need or change. The assumption is that only the trained rheumatologist can provide this service effectively. An audit of the follow-up practice based on criteria agreed by the consultants allows for rationalization of the policy, with the development of a new policy.

The policy would include clear criteria, against which patients should be regularly reviewed or could be seen on a shared-care basis with general practitioners. Given a reduction in the ratio of new to old patients, more new patients could be seen. If this were not enough to deal with the waiting list problem, then a longer-term strategy to increase the medical staff numbers or reduce the referral rate would have to be adopted. The responsibility of the clinical director rests not in the detailed analysis, but in making sure that a clear plan to resolve the problem is brought to fruition while carrying the medical, nursing and managerial staff with the plan.

The above example has components of both short- and medium-term strategic planning. A longer-term plan would involve, for example, the development of a new service either not provided at all, or at present provided in another provider unit but at a level unsatisfactory to either purchasers or patients.

For example, services for both acute and chronic renal dialysis are often provided on a 'regional' basis with all the attendant problems of location, transport for patients and follow-up. This leaves a sub-acute service to be provided by the Trust. It may well be that a more comprehensive service within the Trust to treat local patients would better meet the demands of both patients and hospital. The programme to set up the service, including medical, nursing, technical and support staff, negotiate change of contract and funding and allocate space would require a longer-term strategic plan for implementation over two to three years. In developing strategic plans, the clinical director has a responsibility to develop, on the one hand, the directorate plans in line with those of the Trust, but on the other, to protect the directorate from potential disruption from those same plans. It is essential that the clinical director informs and discusses with the directorate members the development of the strategic plans since they will founder without their support.

ANNUAL BUSINESS PLANNING AND BUDGET SETTING

For most disciplines, budget setting by the Trust will be based on historical funding and predicted activity derived from the previous year's workload. There are very few clinical directors or directorate managers who have sufficient information to build a budget need from zero and for most, costs of care are relatively broad-based. Alongside this are the various types of contracts for services (see Chapter 6).

To date, for the majority, contracts are 'block' with some cost and volume and a few, cost per case. For example, a predominantly emergency service directorate such as general medicine would be likely to have a block contract for the emergency service with a cost and volume for, perhaps, endoscopy services and a cost per case contract for highly specialized, infrequent, cases of, for example, intrahepatic portosystemic shunting. Given that the bulk of the work (85–95%) is emergency demand, which is uncontrolled and at present increasing between 5 and 10% per year nationally, block contracts penalize such disciplines. It is much more straightforward to work with a contract for a negotiated target workload than one that is uncontrollably variable.

The budget should include all elements needed for running the directorate and seeing the patients. It is unusual, however, for total costs to be included in directorate budgets. Given that for most directorates, funding is essentially set from the top, either by the director of finance as lead contract negotiator, or by the purchasers in a command economy where the financing and constraints are delivered top down, it can be very difficult to work within the budget limits and yet deliver the level of care deemed appropriate by health professionals.

It is therefore the duty of the clinical director in developing the business plan, not only to set the objectives for the directorate for the year, but to highlight areas of potential or actual difficulty and develop strategies with the staff for dealing with those problems. These may include changes of practice, redistribution of staff, changes in staffing skill mix, restrictions on care activity, bed closures and redundancies. The analysis of the problems may lead to solutions which require the purchaser to fund, for example, more nursing staff. The development of the plan with the supporting information is the responsibility of the clinical director with his/her directorate manager.

Success with the negotiation solves the problem. Rejection leaves a major organizational difficulty. The solution is either to struggle, or perhaps put patients at some risk with staff increasingly stressed, dissatisfied and with increasing sickness rates (all of which then compound the problem) or to reduce the workload by closing beds, or cutting some other part of the service. This is the most common and often most difficult problem faced by a clinical director.

Closing beds only shifts the problem elsewhere and at the same time may encourage unwelcome enquiry into the running of the directorate. It is a drastic or final measure and should only be resorted to when all other avenues of revenue saving have been explored. The conflict is between being able to deal with patients who are used to care provided to the best of the carer's ability, yet being constrained by funding restrictions which preclude that ethic. Publicity does not necessarily help to resolve the problem. The financial cake is finite. In the end, the clinical director, with his or her colleagues, will have to decide how to ration the service and discuss with the purchasers, general practitioners, and patients/ public, how decisions are reached. These types of problem highlight the conflict between financial control and the medical ethics of 'the best for all patients at all times'.

The year on year reduction in spending, 'cost improvement programmes' and funding reallocation have presented all clinical directors with a need to review their services, not only in terms of looking for savings, but also for changes in practice. These include moves towards day case care, outpatient investigations rather than inpatient, relying more on general practitioners to care for patients at an earlier stage of recovery and even ceasing to provide some services. The latter is an extremely difficult action for any health professional given the ethic of care for all. To cease an activity previously deemed worthwhile needs strong evidence to support such a course of action, otherwise staff understandably feel alienated and frustrated.

In the past, developments in medical care have largely occurred by gradual incorporation of an innovation into working practice without any formal plan being made for costing, benefit analysis, or future funding. With the increasingly restricted budgeting for the acute sector such 'accidental' developments can no longer take place without jeopardizing some element of the existing service.

For example, the introduction of increasingly expensive antibiotics used for neutropenic patients often occurs against a background of variable success with current regimens. The problem lies not in the value of using the newer antibiotics, but in there being no plan for their introduction. It is still not widely perceived that there can be any argument against the use of such agents, yet their introduction threatens not only the rest of the drugs budget but often more direct patient care. The introduction of drugs costing £2000–5000 per week on an unplanned basis is irrational, yet still happens. It stems from that medical ethic of 'the best care possible for the patient' but is now in conflict with the business ethic of clear planning, coordination and justification.

In contrast, the planning for a directorate may be forced top down from the Board, chief executive or purchaser. The decision of a Trust Board to focus on a particular activity with purchasers increasing the demand for that service can have major repercussions for other directorates.

For example, the increasing demand and purchasers' desire for cardiac services means less funds for other activities. Further, the desire for the Trust to provide those services and secure increased income may demand space redistribution at the expense of either an emergency or a less high profile service. The business ethic of income realization is in conflict with the medical ethic of broad-based care provision. Such a concept threatens the clinical director not only intellectually and ethically, but may also ultimately have a direct effect on employment. The decision is beyond the individual clinical director.

BUDGET CONTROL   Even in the best organized directorates, the execution of a plan, which keeps both patient numbers and quality targets within budget, requires precise control. Most Trusts now operate some scheme of retention of underspend and carry forward of overspend year on year. The former is welcome, the latter potentially progressively inevitable. It assumes the budgets were correctly set at the start. Even assuming there were variations in workload, particularly for the emergency services, there is the potential for an overspend beyond the control of the director. The closure of beds, unplanned restriction of drugs use, containment of the use of support services, all threaten the well-being of patients. There has to be a mechanism for the clinical director to seek, with justification, additional funding for such an unpredictable rise in demand.

Of greater difficulty is uncontrolled spending by a consultant, or group of consultants without an agreed plan. This, of course, assumes the directorate, as a whole, agreed to the business plan to start with. It is for many clinical directors extremely difficult to restrict colleagues' activities, against a traditional background of 'clinical freedom'. The tools of audit and outcome analysis, although theoretically attractive, are unfortunately often rejected, probably because they are still seen as threatening. However, properly applied they highlight, not only unsatisfactory practice, but also the good. They are therefore a powerful agent in extending control over the 'maverick' whose practice threatens the rest of the directorate.

The setting of the business plan with the directorate, its regular review and identification of problems at an early stage are key to budget control. The engagement of the whole directorate in the process is paramount. Without such involvement, the problem is rarely solved.

STAFF,   Most clinical directors are responsible for the employment of staff,
PERFORMANCE   other than medical staff, through their managers. Given the
REVIEW AND   development of budgets and with it the responsibility for service
DISCIPLINE   activity, it is right that the clinical director should have control over

the number, skill mix and disposition of staff. This includes not only nursing, but clerical, administrative and support staff. There is, however, wide variation in the level to which development of this role has occurred.

For some, staff employment is the responsibility solely of a staffing or personnel department (human resources department in the current jargon). In others, the directorate takes responsibility for all staff working within the directorate. For the majority, it stops short of catering, portering and domestic staff, either because they are employed through external agencies or because their areas of work cross many directorate boundaries, making single directorate employment wasteful or, alternatively, bureaucratically burdensome.

The management structure of the directorate often includes a nurse manager or senior clinical nurse with responsibility for nursing organization, development, training and recruitment. This arrangement does not remove from the director the responsibility for ensuring appropriate nursing, clinical and support staff for the workload and patient dependency. It does, however, allow the key professional to be responsible for implementation of directorate policies. Further, the devolution of budgets to ward or sector level engages the ward staff in the management process within pre-set and agreed limits. Distant control of manpower levels by the clinical director or the directorate manager, is, in the main, too remote to capture the participation of senior nurses at ward level. The imposition of skill mixes and numbers of staff most often generates resentment and frustration, often with a misconceived sense of a lack of sensitivity to the ward needs.

Most, if not all, would agree that the downward pressure on budgets has been largely met through 'restructuring' the work force. Given that staff form approximately 70% of budget costs in most directorates, it is inevitable that staff costs are a major target for cost savings. The traditional target of the drugs bill is of only marginal benefit given the relatively small component that drug expenditure forms in the total budget. Funding restraints have often resulted in major changes in staffing patterns, both in numbers and skill mix. It is therefore the duty of the directorate to ensure that with any changes, work is still carried out to the set quality standards and where appropriate, to audit care against those standards. Where the funding restrictions mean unacceptable staffing restrictions, with or without bed closures, the clinical director has the responsibility to develop his or her business plan to secure, from either the chief executive or the purchasers, the appropriate budget commensurate with workload demanded and quality standards set.

As an example, emergency admission rates are climbing at an annual rate of between 5% and 10%. Initially, this increasing workload was contained within existing resources (beds, support services and nurses). The continuing cumulative increase, with shortening length of hospital stay, increases the relative dependency of patients, there being fewer patients in recovery or convalescent stage. Moreover, the patients are increasingly at the expensive phase of their care, being discharged before entering any convalescent phase. Their place is immediately taken by another high dependency, high cost patient. The result is an increasingly pressurized group of staff in a directorate with increasing costs beyond the clinical director's immediate control. There are three possible solutions:

1. Do nothing, overspend and have stressed and demoralized staff.
2. Reduce the workload by closing beds: patients suffer directly, as do neighbouring hospitals.
3. Analyse the workload change, the increasing dependency and the related costs to present a business case for increasing the staff numbers and revenue in line with the workload.

If the business plan fails, then the first two options come into play. The key to success is a clear, careful study of the workload increase, the source (both locality and disease) of the increase, the patient dependency, the ability to meet agreed quality standards and staff sickness and resignation ratios. Engaging the purchasers in the study does not necessarily achieve success, but it does share ownership of the problem.

There are three main different aspects of staff management. The first is sickness, the second is poor performance and absenteeism, the third discipline.

The management of sickness is a key part of maintaining the staffing levels without recourse to agency staff. Average sickness levels vary widely between groups of staff, with portering staff having levels of 10–15%, nursing 5–10% and medical staff 2–4%. Given that sickness for a week requires only self-certification, a system of recording and maintaining sickness levels and individual records is essential. The assumption that outside agency staff will automatically replace the absentee is no longer realistic. Budgets often do not allow for more than an average rate of 4% sick leave and, more significantly, it is seen as more than a pair of hands. Staff who take persistent sickness leave need to be reviewed, not accusingly, but in a constructive manner. The involvement of the occupational health department is critical in managing the problem, not least for the member of staff. Managing long-term sickness is most delicate, but ignoring it is damaging to the directorate and individual. The ultimate solution is retirement on health grounds.

Those who perform poorly disadvantage their colleagues. The disciplining of such individuals requires clear documentation of the problems and failure to fulfil tasks, appropriate counselling and ultimately, if there is no improvement, dismissal. It is clear that an understanding of employment law and a recognition of the need to give the member of staff an opportunity to improve are essential. It is a disagreeable task, but failure to tackle it leads to disaffection in the whole group.

Errors of judgement, negligent actions and failure of care should be dealt with promptly, objectively and expeditiously, based on information received from as many sources as possible. As with poor performers, the best course is often to get assistance from the director of personnel (human resources). Where appropriate, the early involvement of the proper person prevents later difficulties.

In the end, the clinical director is responsible for the welfare and management of directorate staff.

I have already discussed some aspects of formal discipline, but not those of informal discipline. Informal discipline is normally devolved to an intermediate level, for example, a ward sister for nursing staff, a senior secretary or general assistant for clerical staff. Management of the problems at ward or office level reduces the threat to staff, yet gives the opportunity for early resolution and better integration of teams. When this fails, then the more senior line manager takes over. Unfortunately, all too often little training in staff management is given, in particular in appraisal and performance review. These processes are important in averting habits or performance trends which would otherwise result in a disciplinary action.

The management of medical staff is more difficult since most of them have been trained to act independently on the basis of their own expertise and resent criticism (even when constructive).

Dealing with the poor performance of an individual member of medical staff is initially the clinical director's responsibility. Indeed, for many Trusts the clinical director now has to carry out appraisals and reviews at intervals, for most, of three years with a review of job plans each year.

The universities have, for some time, appraised staff at all levels, but largely sporadically. Only junior medical staff have had regular reviews. The introduction of appraisals and performance review should bring with it a two-way process between appraiser and appraised in a constructive dialogue to reach objectives for personal development.

The performance review is, however, difficult to disentangle from the appraisal and is, by its nature, threatening. It requires training and skill to avoid a destructive, non-productive confrontation. It is, however, a major opportunity to deal with difficulties before they become problems. Nonetheless, there are those whose activities require change: for example, the consultant who persistently ignores protocols for patient admission, drug policies agreed within the directorate, or whose supervision of junior staff is unsatisfactory. Unfortunately, for many appraisal is a token gesture, a system of going through the motions without real benefit.

Although discredited in industry, properly applied it can be an invaluable personal development tool.

The tackling of such seemingly simple problems is surprisingly difficult for a clinical manager. Dealing with a peer in these circumstances, no matter how well justified, will almost inevitably be interpreted as a confrontation. For most, there has to be some face-saver, a route to keep dignity. Often the delegation of some directorate responsibility, for example, setting an educational programme for junior staff, not only highlights the problem area, but allows the consultant to emerge with credit.

There are those, however, who do not respond to any peer pressure. It is then that resort to the medical director or the 'Three Wise Men' (the independent group of consultants within the Trust appointed to tackle such personal conduct) is appropriate. Ultimately, the failure of a doctor to fulfil his or her contract leads to the use of disciplinary procedures as set out in terms and conditions of service, with dismissal being the final sanction.

To ignore incompetence, poor performance, or even negligence, is no longer justifiable, acceptable or ethical. The recent case of the clinical director brought before the General Medical Council and disciplined for failing to take action concerning an incompetent colleague is a clear statement of a clinical director's responsibilities. Early intervention, unpleasant though it may be, avoids such disasters.

QUALITY ASSURANCE   Quality assurance has become a key part of the Health Service. It applies equally to the simplest service, such as ward food delivery, as to the cost and outcome of the most difficult surgical procedure. The development of national standards for waiting times is a small but often resented part of quality assurance. Resentment comes from the belief of health professionals that they are attempting to provide the highest quality care at all times. Nonetheless, there is a wide ranging opportunity to practise and to develop standards for care to which most, if not all, can subscribe. For example, bed sores remain a problem in many highly dependent patients. A standard might be set that no patient develops a bed sore. Analysis of what is actually happening leads to a care plan which prevents sores occurring, without necessarily increasing nursing demands.

Another example would be the number of times a patient moves wards during their stay. Many organizations work on progression from high to low dependency areas. This may, or may not, be best practice, but if a standard is set independent of what is current practice, then a review of that practice becomes inevitable. If there is a reduction of beds in emergency acute specialties with an increasing workload, it is likely that the specialty will overflow into other areas. It is necessary to place the most sick where the equipment and nursing skills match the need (concentration of nurses and equipment giving better outcome than when scattered). The patients are admitted to the high skill and dependency wards and then moved as dependency decreases. It is usual for the pre-convalescent patient to be relocated out to other areas. The collection of the data showing number of moves (against the predetermined standard), the nursing and portering hours involved and the difficulties of care (medical and nursing) provide the basis for a business case, either to change the admission policy or to increase the dedicated facilities.

Quality assurance now forms a key part of all business plans but nonetheless, a large amount of work still needs to be done to approach the concept of 'right first time, every time, on time'. The management of complaints is a key part of quality assurance. The starting point is ideally that no complaint should occur, but if it does, each complaint should be analysed, just like an accident report, for the factors that led to the complaint. A clear policy for handling complaints must be formulated, a policy which all employees understand. The objective is a clear response within a short time addressing the complaint with, if necessary, an explana-tion of any further stages, or avenues for the complainant to pursue. Analysis of the accumulated data for both complaints and quality assurance problems should lead to problem identification and eradication. Ignoring, or simply filing the completed procedure, has value only for the single episode.

A further part of quality assurance is risk assessment and manage-ment. This includes not only clinical risk, but risk to employees, patients and public. To foster a positive staff attitude to quality and risk avoidance, a system for non-threatening reporting of incidents must be developed. In the past, only clear accidents have been reported, but a change to the reporting of incidents or 'near misses' allows for the development of change to avert the more serious event and should be encouraged.

Audit is not often seen as a tool of quality assurance, but the development of clinical audit, with the involvement of all health professionals, has broadened the remit. The assessment of practice or outcome against present standards with modification of practice and subsequent reassessment based on the results of audits (closing the loop) is a vital process in improving practice within an established field. Without audit, the assumption of 'good perfor-mance' remains untested. With it, confidence in the quality of the service follows.

EDUCATION, RESEARCH AND DEVELOPMENT

Education and training are not yet directly within the remit of the clinical director's responsibility. While the clinical tutor has the responsibility, on behalf of the postgraduate dean, to see that there are educational supervisors and training programmes for junior medical staff, the director is responsible for the provision and standard of the programmes. Trust hospitals now have contracts with the postgraduate dean for the training of junior medical staff and the clinical directors, through the chief executive, are accountable for that training. The development of this responsibility allows programmes to be tailored to directorate specialty needs but does not, and should not, preclude collaboration across directorates. For teaching hospital Trusts there is the added responsibility of providing undergraduate teaching and most now include a clear commitment to teaching within the job plans of their consultants. The clinical director is responsible for seeing that the directorate fulfils these obligations, especially since the Trust has a contract through Service Increment for Teaching and Research (SIFTR) for the provision of undergraduate education. Wherever such education takes place, the same principles apply.

Training and education are more clearly defined for medical staff than others, but with the implementation of the NHS Working Paper 10, training programmes and staff development are necessary for all staff. Whether or not there is a Trust or hospital budget for training, the director has a duty to foster the training and development of staff employed in the organization.

Research and development have similarly been raised to a new level. For those receiving SIFTR, there is a need to account for and justify the 'R' component of that funding. Most Trust hospitals will have a research and development committee, but the director should encourage NHS research within the directorate. This is probably best accomplished by giving lead responsibility for encouraging and fostering NHS research to a consultant, but too often the needs of the nursing and professions allied to medicine are ignored. The whole directorate should participate in research though superficially the time spent on research may appear to be in conflict with patient care. Nonetheless it is becoming an essential part of the Trust and directorate activity.

EXTERNAL RELATIONSHIPS

Good relationships with other directorates are an essential part of a director's role. Without them, conflict and confrontation will arise. The most usual cause of conflict is the perceived commandeering of beds notionally allocated to another directorate which then interferes with the 'official' bed holder's ability to fulfil contracts. The establishment of clear communication lines and discussion of problems, preferably in anticipation of the event, is the key to cooperation.

Another potential difficulty is the relationship with outside organizations. A common one is that with the pharmaceutical industry for drug trials. Traditionally, these have been carried out in NHS space and time with no income generated for the hospital. Looked at objectively, this appears at first to be 'free-good' for the industry, but in fact this may not be so. Within the current commercial climate, the main aim should be at least 'no cost' to the Trust. At present, most companies pay for investigations and pharmacy use. The benefit to the Trust is in the provision of the trial drug which relieves the cost of prescriptions. In contrast, the unseen effect is the future potential influence of the trial on prescribing habits, which could turn into a significant drain on resources.

To avoid possible conflicts, a number of Trusts have set up clinical trial units for the sole purpose of undertaking trials in all clinical phases. These units are clearly managed as income generating business units with fees for the use of the facilities, which are thus recouped from the trial. This has put such studies on a much firmer business arrangement without compromising the ability to carry out such trials. It has also helped to clarify patients' participation in such studies and separated this from their routine care.

Perhaps the most difficult are the relationships with outside organizations for whom contracts are carried out. It is common for 'waiting list initiatives' to be sub-contracted to the private hospital sector where the work is often carried out by the same consultant who would have done it within the Trust hospital. The potential for a conflict of interest arises when consultants act as advisers to private hospitals, who then compete for the business of the Trust. Such consultants are not only jeopardizing the income for the Trust hospital, but, by implication, their own salaries. If the work is directed to the private sector, there is no need for them in the Trust hospital. In recognition of this, most Trust hospitals have developed guidelines for consultants to avoid such conflicts. The director has a responsibility to ensure such potential conflicts do not arise.

Finally, industry (pharmaceutical, equipment manufacturers, consumable suppliers) are now developing schemes for providing whole units (for example, renal units) to Trusts on a service contract basis. This is very often at cheaper initial cost and allows the unit or Trust to fulfil or attract contracts. Once established, such contracts can be very difficult to escape. The contracts require meticulous attention to detail, not only for the present but also to take account of future developments. For example, if a company is contracted to provide a renal unit and key advances are developed by a rival company, there has to be the capacity to absorb that development, which is clearly a business threat to the initial service company. It is inevitable that business considerations will threaten the medical ethic of the best care available with the funding available.

As the links with the private sector develop, not only for patient care, but for financing, the imperatives of business are in danger of subsuming the medical ethics of patient care and must be resisted forcefully.

SUMMARY

Clinical directors have responsibility for:

♦ Developing and implementing the strategic and annual business plan.

♦ Ensuring the delivery of services to the quality standards set.

♦ Managing (and sometimes disciplining) staff, including medical staff.

♦ Making sure that educational, training and research contracts are fulfilled.

FURTHER READING

♦ Bank, J. (1992), *The Essence of Total Quality Management*. Prentice Hall.

♦ Bowman, C. (1990), *The Essence of Strategic Management*. Prentice Hall.

♦ Fielding, P. and Benham, P. C. (Eds). (1990), *Surviving in General Management*. Macmillan Education.

♦ Nelson, M. (1989), *Managing Health Care Professionals*. Chapman & Hall, London.

♦ Pettigrew, A., Ferlie, E. and McKee, L. (1992) *Shaping Strategic Change*. Sage Publications.

GLOSSARY

Average Specialty Cost   The total cost of running a specialty service divided by the total number of episodes of care delivered by that service.

Bar (Gantt) Chart   A means of effectively communicating a project programme. It contains a series of tasks and their projected start and finish times.

Block Contracts   A form of contract which specifies a given number of treatments to be provided at an average price.

Budget   A financial plan covering an operation for a fixed period of time.

Business Case   The formal proposal, as defined in the Capital Investment Manual for seeking approval for new projects, describing the proposals and assessing their commercial and financial attractiveness.

Business Process Re-engineering   Management jargon for improving the operational effectiveness (cost, service and quality) of an organization by re-thinking key processes, systems, tasks and jobs.

Capital Charge   Financing costs which combine the interest costs on the capital and depreciation to enable assets to be replaced in the future.

Case Mix   The numbers of different types of case within a given contract.

Clinical Directorate   That portion of a provider unit managed by a Clinical Director and his or her support staff. It may be of varying size and budget and may contain several different specialties or service departments.

Commissioning Agency   The purchaser function of a Health Authority.

Cost Centre   A responsibility centre within an enterprise, the performance of which is assessed in terms of the service it provides and the costs that it incurs in providing that service.

Critical Path Analysis   This deconstructs a project into discrete tasks with each task assessed for time duration and other tasks which must be completed prior to being able to start this task. The tasks are then assembled using critical path analysis which enables the following to be calculated:

♦ The critical path for the project
♦ The overall duration of the project
♦ The earliest and latest finish times for each task without affecting the overall duration of the project.

Direct Cost   A cost which relates directly to a particular activity.

Directly Managed Unit   A provider unit which does not have Trust status and is therefore directly managed by a Health Authority.

External Financing Limit (EFL)   The net amount of money a Trust is allowed to borrow/repay to the Department of Health.

Finished/Completed Consultant Episode   A programme of care from the point of admission to the point of discharge whilst the patient is under the care of one consultant.

Fixed Cost   That element of cost which remains the same despite a change in activity.

Float Time   The amount of delay possible in a particular task without affecting the overall completion date of the project.

GP Fundholder   A GP practice who hold a budget for services which they can purchase from hospitals and other providers of health and social care on behalf of their patients.

Indirect Cost   Costs not controlled directly by a manager but incurred in performing a given level of activity.

Interest Bearing Debt (IBD)   That part of the Trust's balance sheet for which it has to pay interest charges to the Department of Health.

Likelihood Ratio   Ratio of the proportion of those with a positive test who have the disease (true positive rate) to those with a positive test who do not have the disease (false positive rate).

Managed Market   An approach to the organization of services which has some of the characteristics of a market place (purchasers, providers, contracts, prices), but in which procedures exist to regulate or control the operation of the market rather than simply relying on free market forces.

Marginal Cost   The additional cost of providing a given extra level of activity.

Medical (Clinical) Audit   Medical audit is the critical analysis of the provision of medical care including the procedures used for diagnosis and treatment, the use of resources and the resulting outcome for the patient. It is usually carried out by medical staff. A Clinical Audit is the same process carried out by a range of health care professionals including medical staff and looks more widely at the whole experience of the patient including medical care.

Net Present Value (NPV)   The NPV is a three step financial calculation:

1. Calculate the actual cash flows in each year of the project.

2. Discount cash flows in future years by a fixed percentage every year.
3. Sum the discounted cash flows to give the NPV.

The NPV is a single £ number which accounts for the fact that a £ today is worth more than a £ in the future. The higher the NPV, the more attractive the project.

Opportunity Cost   The benefit given up in the best alternative use of the resources.

Outsourcing   Getting other organizations in the public or private sector to perform certain tasks, often under a multi-year contract, e.g. cleaning, catering and, more recently, laboratory services.

Overhead Cost   Cost which is incurred irrespective of activity in the short term.

Parsonnet Score   A weighted index of case severity used in the assessment of outcome of cardiac surgery. The score incorporates in an additive model scores for disease severity (e.g. measures of left ventricular function) and co-morbidity (e.g. diabetes, hypertension, obesity).

Payback Period   This is the number of years required to repay the initial capital outlay for a project from the revenue savings made as a result of the initial capital investment without discounting future cash flows.

Positive Predictive Value   Proportion of those with a positive test who have the disease.

Post Project Evaluation (PPE)   A formal system of evaluating the success of a project and the lessons to be learned for future projects after project completion.

Public Dividend Capital (PDC)   That part of the Trust's balance sheet for which it has to pay a dividend to the Department of Health.

Quality Adjusted Life Years (QALYs)   A measurement of health status which integrates in a single index life years gained with changes in quality of life. QALYs are used as a measure of benefit in cost utility analysis.

Randomized Controlled Trial (RCT)   An epidemiological experiment in which subjects in a study population are allocated randomly into 'study' and 'control' groups to receive or not receive experimental therapeutic or preventive intervention. The strengths of the RCT are random allocation (minimizing the risk of unsuspected confounding) and blinded (or masked) subjects and observers (minimizing these potential sources of bias).

Resource Management   The concept which was central to the Resource Management Initiative: it links quality of care, clinical activity levels and resource consumption in the same management process. Information management and technology is required to provide accurate and timely information for management purposes.

Semi Fixed Cost   A cost which is fixed for a limited amount of additional activity but variable once that limit has been reached.

Sensitivity (of a test)   Proportion of those with the disease in whom the particular test is positive.

Specificity (of a test)   Proportion of those without the disease in whom the particular test is negative.

Standing Financial Instructions   The financial regulations which govern the workings of an NHS Trust or Health Authority.

Statute   Government legislation.

Tort   The legal term for breach of legal duty, other than under contract, with liability for damages.

Total Quality Management   An approach to quality management originating in the private sector which aims to be comprehensive.

Trust Board   The Board which has overall responsibility for management of an NHS Trust. It is made up of a Chairperson appointed by the Secretary of State and an equal number of Executives and Non-Executive Directors, up to five of each. The Executive Directors must by statute include the Chief Executive, the Finance Officer, and the Nursing and Medical Directors. The Non-Executive Directors are usually appointed for their expertise in other fields; they often include business people, accountants and lawyers.

Variable Cost   The element of cost which moves with changes in activity.

Virement   The movement of budget from one budget heading to another.

INDEX

Note: terms explained in the Glossary are indicated by **bold page numbers**; text in Boxes, Figures and Tables by *italic page numbers*. Index entries are arranged in letter-by-letter order (ignoring spaces).